T0368313

CUSTOMIZE...
don't minimize...
YOUR RETIREMENT©

"7 Paths to Explore Possibilities, Choices, and
Your Future Happiness"

Diane B. Burman and Donald C. Strauss

c**Y**r Publishing

First published by AuthorHouse 7/2/2009
AuthorHouse™
1663 Liberty Drive
Bloomington, IN 47403
www.authorhouse.com
Phone: 1-800-839-8640

ISBN: 978-1-4389-2816-6 (sc)

Library of Congress Control Number: 2009904344

Printed in the United States of America
This book is printed on acid-free paper.

Previously Printed in the United States of America by CYR Publishing 2008

Illustrations and cover by Brandon McGruder
Photo images including cover images: www.ablestock.com

ACKNOWLEDGEMENTS

A very special thank-you to Shirley Brussell, the original co-founder of the RetireRight Center, whose support, love and caring over the years, helped make possible this accomplishment.

We would like to thank the following people for their careful reading of the manuscript and their comments and suggestions:
- Michele Baldwin
- Donald Double
- Eileen Keeler
- Art Koff
- Pam Passis
- Loretta Foxman Polsky
- Janet Rand
- Doug Seville
- Linda Strauss Stern
- Rachel and Philip Strauss
- Marjorie Share Swerdlow
- Dennis Zavac

We would also like to acknowledge the following people for their advice, counsel and support:
- Lori and Guy Burman
- Nancy Cashen
- Francine Dines
- Marjorie Ellenbogen
- Allison Burman Gordon
- Susan Jacobson
- Sol Levine
- Bill Welter
- Jeff Williams

In addition, we would like to recognize Richard N. Bolles, Marc Freedman, Richard Lieder, Harry R. Moody, Ph.D., John E. Nelson, Stephen Post, and George Vaillant, whose important work in the field of retirement planning influenced our thinking.

We would also like to thank the Community Renewal Society in Chicago for their support and for providing us a venue for meetings and conferences

WE WOULD LIKE TO DEDICATE THIS BOOK TO OUR SPOUSES:

A special thank-you to my wife, Jan Strauss, for her support and patience in all matters of time and place.

A big thank-you to my "retired" husband, Dr. Shelly Burman, whose forbearance and encouragement are greatly appreciated.

TABLE OF CONTENTS

Index of Exercises by Chapter

INTRODUCTION

"CUSTOMIZE...Don't Minimize...YOUR RETIREMENT"©

We know you are questioning your future and wondering what is around the next curve. There are lots of advisors telling Boomers how to prepare for their future years. Most of that advice is centered on one's financial well-being, not one's mental and emotional well-being.

When the authors themselves were debating what to do in their own retirement, they searched for advice and counsel from books and other sources. The vast majority of information available was centered on financial planning. It is well to heed this advice, but we felt that something was missing. Money is definitely important, but there is more to the retirement years. And, as we became more frustrated with not finding information that could meet our needs, we asked friends and colleagues what their experience has been on the topic of the non-financial aspects of retirement. We discovered that they too had been struggling with the same sorts of questions:

- How do I make better decisions about the future?
- How do I get my future "on track"?
- How do I adjust my housing to my changing needs?
- Who will I be in this new phase of my life?
- Will I be valued if I no longer work?

1

- Will I be fulfilled if I really "gear down"?
- How do I turn my dreams into reality?
- What will make me happy?
- Will my family and friends react favorably to my plans for my future lifestyle?
- How do I adjust my finances to correspond to my needs?

We then realized that people were hungry for information and advice about their future and we decided to meet this need with the creation of this book.

The authors developed over 80 exercises that you can <u>choose to use</u> in creating a future plan for yourself. **These exercises are available to you so that you can pick and choose the ones most suited to your own life situation.** No need to feel overwhelmed by the number of exercises. Some of these may not feel relevant to your experience or lifestyle. You can just choose to skip those and go on to others. We know you have limited time so we have designed the book and the exercises for self-discovery and as a catalyst to discussion with the important people in your life.

Both authors have extensive background in the field of human resources, and especially in career management and career development. As coaches and advisors to hundreds of clients over the years, we realize how difficult it is to manage significant transitions in one's life. Moving into the retirement years can be an extremely challenging transition. Whether one chooses to continue working, to change careers, to try out the "leisure lifestyle" or to brave re-entry into a classroom situation, one may feel the fear of the unknown. In addressing the future years, one must face concerns, not only about finances, but also about new identity, structuring one's time, making new friends and dealing with aging. How comforting it is to have a guide during those times.

Our goal in writing this book has been to help individuals deal with their uneasiness in attempting to answer some of the following questions:

- Who am I?
- Who would I like to be?
- Who are really my friends?
- Should I live near the children?
- Do I stay in my current home?
- Will I work or not work?
- If I work, should I work full time or part time?
- What do I do with my time?
- Is it all right just to enjoy the luxury of doing nothing?
- Should I have a new life purpose?
- Will volunteering satisfy me?
- Should I have a back-up plan if health or economic conditions change?

As people are contemplating retirement, or are already retired, these are the types of questions rattling around in their heads.

You are <u>unique</u>. No two people have the same backgrounds and experiences, the same dreams or aspirations. As individuals who also have had to deal with this transformation, we, the authors, want to help you attain your own <u>customized</u> happy retirement.

This book strives to be unique in that it:
- Is easy to read.
- Is easy to understand.
- Raises more than just money questions; it raises questions that drive your life.
- Makes you into a hands-on user, not just a passive reader through the use of 80+ exercises.
- Allows you to jump between exercises and chapters.
- Allows you to have fun and not feel constrained to complete all the exercises or chapters.
- Encourages you to work with friends and relatives, or perhaps a coach, in discussing and completing the exercises.

In the first chapter, "Envision Your Ideal Retirement," you will be introduced to the chapter topics and invited to experience some of the exercises. This will help you get "your toe in the water." "Envision Your Ideal Retirement" is the first of the "7 Paths to Explore Possibilities, Choices and Your Future Happiness," i.e. the need to develop/envision a set of clear goals, a vision, or a specific dream for your retirement.

The remaining 6 Paths follow the format of the book and deal with: 1. The need to complete one's "Financial Picture…Making it a Masterpiece; 2. The need to "Keep in Shape;" 3. The need to plan what "Being at Home" will look like in retirement; 4. The need to keep "Vitalizing Relationships" throughout your life; 5. The need to redefine work in retirement so it feels like "Work is no Longer Work" and 6. The need to deal with future leisure time so it is "Time to Do Good and/or for Good Times" (so it can include time for developing a creative lifestyle, volunteering, or traveling.)

Retirement planning differs from other life planning which you have been doing. This new phase of your life typically involves:
- Seeing your financial picture shift from accumulating savings to spending your savings and perhaps living on a more limited or structured budget,
- Having uncommitted time available, not defined by or structured by your occupation.
- Finding that maintenance of health could become a larger factor affecting your activities over time.
- Adjusting to new demands or requests from others (particularly family and friends).

As you attempt to gain a new balance in your lifestyle, uncommitted time can provide an opportunity to gain true fulfillment in your retirement, or, in contrast, cause a sense of malaise and discomfort.

We realize that each person needs time to reflect, examine his/her unique current circumstances, explore future possibilities, evaluate different action scenarios and plan specific actions to attain a desirable lifestyle in this next phase of your life. We, therefore, encourage you to take your time with the exercises; don't rush through them. Concentrate on the ones that make the most sense for you or the ones that seem most important at this particular time. Discuss them with the people in your life who are important to you and with those who could be most helpful.

Some people make decisions quickly based on their values and beliefs; others need to examine facts before making a decision. Both decision-making styles may benefit from the exercises and information in this book. Those who prefer facts and want to dig deep before deciding on an action plan will benefit from the information in the narrative portion of the book, as well as completing many of the exercises. Those who arrive at decisions quickly, may benefit from answering the questions in the exercises to substantiate or confirm their previously held opinions.

A DREAM + A PLAN + A DEADLINE + TAKING ACTION =
FINDING YOUR OWN PERSONAL FUTURE HAPPINESS

So here it is…a user-friendly compendium of materials that discusses the world of pre-retirement planning, covering an array of topics from looking at your savings and future financial well-being to evaluating your relationships, health or available time…facts wrapped around the need to do self-analysis…in distinct pieces (exercises) that you can do at your leisure, over time.

We hope you take the challenge and move ahead with your planning, finding the materials contained in this book to be both stimulating and insightful. In conclusion, it's up to you… no one else can walk in your shoes or do what needs to be done to bring about the lifestyle that you will choose for yourself. Invest the time and thought and, be assured, you will be rewarded for having taken this initiative; so, get ready to customize your own unique retirement.

Diane B. Burman
Donald C. Strauss

Please note that The RetireRight Center is also there to help. This <u>non-profit</u> consulting company in Chicago exists to provide training workshops and individualized coaching on the topic of transitioning into retirement. The RetireRight Center is available as an adjunct to doing the work of planning on your own. You can learn more about the Center at www.retirerightcenter.org **or call 312-673-3842.**

CHAPTER 1

PATH 1: ENVISION YOUR IDEAL RETIREMENT

"Would you tell me please which way I ought to go from here?" asked Alice.
"That depends a good deal on where you want to get to," said the Cheshire Cat.
"I don't much care where…"
"Then it doesn't matter which way you go."
"…so long as I get somewhere," said Alice.
"Oh, you're sure to do that if only you walk long enough," sneered the Cat.
Through the Looking-Glass, Lewis Carroll (1832-1898) English author, mathematician, logician, Anglican clergyman, photographer

Welcome to **"Customize Your Retirement."**© We know that you have opened this book to find out more about yourself and discover ways to enhance the next stage of your life.

The **book** contains:

A set of 8 chapters that are intended to review the many aspects of retirement, as well as providing self-discovery "thinker tools" (exercises) to help you evaluate options, opportunities and plans for retirement. These chapters are entitled: (1) "Envision Your Ideal Retirement," (2) "The Financial Picture…Make It A Masterpiece," (3) "Keeping in Shape," (4) "Being at Home," (5) "Vitalizing Relationships," (6) "Work is No Longer Work," (7) "Time to Do Good and For Good Times," (8) "Your Action Plan."

In this chapter, you will have the opportunity to:

- Learn about how the book is organized and what to expect.
- Think about some of the challenges and choices that await you in this next phase of your life.
- Dream a little about what you'd like to plan for in your retirement.
- Create a vision of the ideal retirement for you.

Before we outline what to expect in your journey through **"Customize Your Retirement"**© we would like to give you some background. As a likely member of the generation labeled "Boomer," you have probably read about the great demographic trend in our society; a great many people are retiring earlier and people are living longer. This presents wonderful opportunities for someone in your age group, and also many stimulating challenges. This may prove to be scary for some folks, but we are convinced that the more planning you do now, the less worrisome the coming years will be. The opportunity to find new outlets for your talents, to work in activities that will prove to be satisfying and fulfilling and to build strong relationships with those people who are most important to you, will fill your "second half" with purpose and meaning. WAKE UP AND DREAM is our motto and we have built **"Customize Your Retirement"**© to assist you in finding your own personal dreams and acting on them.

Consider This

Just to get you in the mood, see how much you know about the world of retirement by choosing true or false for each of the following statements. The answers will follow each statement. We think you will be surprised.

1. About 2,500 individuals are reaching age 60 every day.
   (False: About 8,000 reach age 60 daily.)

2. About 40% of those retiring plan to work in retirement.
   (False: The most recent statistics show that 79% plan to work in retirement.)

3. Retirees look forward to living a "Life of Leisure" in retirement.
   (False: Most Boomers want to make a difference in retirement, i.e. volunteering, accomplishing an unfinished dream, working in some capacity, gaining fulfillment, etc.)

4. Social Security is not the primary source of income to most retirees.
   (False: Today Social Security is still the primary income source for retirees.)

5. Most people who are contemplating retirement plan to relocate to a new residence within a year or two of retirement.
   (False: Most entering retirement remain in their present residence and favor being close to their children.)

6. Most Boomers will have pensions when they retire.
   (False: Most Boomers will not have pensions.)

7. Most retirees can finally relax from family caretaking responsibilities beyond caring only for themselves.
   (False: Most retirees will need to help their aging parents, adult children, grandchildren, or other family members.)

8. Most retirees retire at age 65; and only once.
   (False: Most Boomers and others soon to retire will retire before age 65 at least once, then return to the workforce, retire a second and even perhaps a third time.)

9. Men have an easier time retiring than women do.
   (False: Men have a substantially more difficult time retiring because they lose their occupational identity and the scheduling of their day that revolves around their previous occupation. It has been said many times that men need to learn how to use their Leisure Time in retirement.)

10. Planning for the day one could be disabled or hampered by poor health is a major consideration in planning ahead.
    (False: Individuals fail to really plan for a future hampered by poor health; they tend not to purchase long-term care insurance because it is viewed as being so expensive.)

11. Most retirees have a pretty clear vision of what they will do when they retire.
    (False: Typically those planning retirement in a year or two plan vacations and travel, but not whether they will work, or how they will use their unscheduled leisure time on an ongoing basis. Further, they usually don't carefully examine the amount of money they will need to live on over the years to come.)

12. Those planning retirement generally have sufficient insurance to address their future needs.
    (False: Typically, they lack sufficient long-term care insurance, insurance for burial, and in many cases sufficient coverage for their medical needs.)

13. "Monte Carlo simulations" for investment and retirement planning and other calculators are best left to experts for advising perspective retirees on how to manage their portfolios.

(True: They should use a professional financial consultant to advise them from an independent perspective. And, if you do not know what a Monte Carlo simulation is, don't worry. Financial consultants should know. But for your information, it is often used to determine allocation of retirement funds and how long these funds will last.)

14. Not having enough money to live on in retirement is the single biggest concern for prospective retirees.
(True: Money is a major issue that needs to be addressed as it really does impact choices. Imbedded in the statements above are other considerations that also impact one's lifestyle choices; issues such as one's new identity, planning for future health needs; housing choices; using one's time; maintaining and building quality relationships; etc.)

So, how did you do? Was this exercise informative? Were you aware of some of the trends taking place in the larger society? Now that you are warmed up, we would like to introduce you to **"Customize Your Retirement."**©

Retirement...Whose definition is it really?

Retirement is an interesting word to define. It is so dependent on an individual's life situation that we would be hard-pressed to try and establish parameters for this very elusive concept. The root of the word literally means "to pull back" and, as we are all finding out, now that the life span has lengthened considerably and people are remaining healthy much longer, very few people want to pull back. The leisure lifestyle, which was prevalent in previous generations, is almost going the way of the Edsel. For instance:

- A colleague of ours was finishing up his projects. His wife had technically retired 18 months before. Now he is down to the end of one project, and she has been pulled back into work. He said that she still wanted more. So, he said... this is her retirement, not mine, and we are out of synch, but this is important to her.
- Another two friends who were executives at a large corporation retired at age 40. Retired? They don't need to work for financial reasons. One had a child, and is doing things pro bono, but is now also earning some money; the other has started two businesses since his retirement 2 years ago.
- An aunt of ours, who was widowed recently, decided to change her lifestyle and share her house with her widowed sister and together they would run the house as a bed and breakfast. This allowed them to enjoy each other's company, as well as maintaining a source of income.

So...what is retirement? Retirement used to mean crossing a bridge to Florida. No more. As people live longer there are more opportunities, the opportunity to create a new life at any age; whether that means your 40's, 50's, 60's, 70's, even your 80's. Look at examples of people who have or are currently re-inventing themselves and finding new beginnings...Paul Newman, Grandma Moses, John McCain, Robert Redford, Donald Trump, Eleanor Roosevelt, Nelson Mandela, Pope John Paul, etc. So what is the next phase for you? The phase that offers you the time and ability to really deviate from the past and do what makes you happy.

Retire happy

This first chapter, entitled "Envision Your Ideal Retirement," encourages you to build a **vision** of your ideal retirement. What will my "new life" be like? What will change in my work life, in my family life? This is the time to free associate, "sky's the limit," imagine possibilities. What things come to mind at this stage? Think positive; eliminate regrets about the past. What will be new, different? What will be the same? What are the opportunities; what are the challenges?

 To help you seek answers to these questions, please turn to **Exercise 1 (page 19)**, "Introducing 'Customize Your Retirement'©" . This exercise is designed to help you focus your planning efforts and determine what information you need to move ahead and what topics are most pressing at this point in time. It will also help you use the book most effectively.

Now that you have clarified some of your retirement goals and discovered what chapters in the book may be most helpful to you, we can move on to the next topic.

Chapter 2, "The Financial Picture…Making it a Masterpiece," helps you to understand your **financial** situation and to set financial goals. What are some of the financial issues I need to be thinking about? Do I have a financial advisor and, if not, have I thought about why I might need one? What will be sources of future income? What will be my expenses in the future? Do I need to do estate planning? What are vital papers and forms I need to complete? Is my spouse or significant other on the same page with me in making financial decisions? Chapter 2, "The Financial Picture, Making It a Masterpiece" is designed to guide you through some of these questions and assist you in finding answers.

 Everyone's financial picture in retirement is different. There is no one-size fits all. You will need as much detail as possible about your goals, when you want to retire, where and how you want to live, and what you want to leave behind. It's a complex financial "stew" requiring people to make tough decisions on spending, saving and risk. And the calculations need to be adjusted as times, needs and assets change. Most people need to set priorities and make tradeoffs.

Consider This

Chapter 3, "Keeping in Shape," helps you understand the effect of **health and fitness** on your future plans. You will take a look at your current fitness level; what kinds of nutritional choices you make; how you have fun keeping fit. You will begin to analyze what the stressors are in your life and how to avoid or eliminate them so that you are aware of how to maintain your mental as well as your physical health. Working with your spouse or partner, you can begin to make plans about how to build and maintain a healthy lifestyle. Sometimes the health issues of a loved one become an unexpected priority. How will you respond? What are your roles and responsibilities when a family member is stricken? These and other questions need to be pondered and planned for.

Moving into **Chapter 4,** "Being at Home," gives you the opportunity to begin to plan for your **housing** needs. You can start to understand the issues and become knowledgeable about options. There are different stages in the retirement years and understanding what they are can help you plan more effectively. Location and geography play a part in your planning. Do you want to be near your children and grandchildren? Are there health issues that will make it more imperative for you to live in a particular location? How does the cost of living in certain locales affect your planning? Can you stay in your current home, even if your health changes, and what would that require in terms of reconstruction or other adjustments? What are the housing possibilities in any of the cities or locales you prefer? Chapter 4, "Being at Home in Retirement" will take you through some of the challenges, rewards and choices available in housing options.

Chapter 5, "Vitalizing Relationships" gets you thinking about the **relationships** in your life. First is the relationship with yourself. What is your new identity? How will you label yourself? You will begin to understand the wide impact of the role changes in your own life and how those impact your sense of self. As you work on redefining new roles and relationships through a self-assessment process, you will begin to understand what the challenges and changes may be in the coming years. You will be making choices about friends and family. You may need to learn new skills in handling these changing relationships. You may have to revise your communication style and learn how to make and keep new friends and deal more effectively with family members. This is an exciting time and full of opportunities for personal growth and development.

As you move into **Chapter 6** "Work is No Longer Work," you will find many questions that you may want to ponder and to plan how you will respond to these questions. These questions will begin with helping you to understand your need to work; what are your options; what are the barriers to your choices of work; what are the opportunities that arise. You will begin to discover why you want to work and what you want in a job. Do you want to continue in your current career with only scheduling changes to allow you more free time? Do you want to work full time or part time? What are the job options and opportunities? Based on a good self-assessment, you will be more in touch with how you want to approach your work life in the coming years.

One of the keys to determining the type of work you want to be doing is your own personal set of values. A value is something that is important, desirable or useful to you as an individual. Values may vary, evolve or simply disappear as we move through life stages. Now, as you are planning the next stage of your life is a good time to re-evaluate your values when making decisions.

Please turn to **Exercise 2 (page 21)**, "Your Values Clarification Opportunity" to begin the process of researching what is important to you.

As you pondered your current values, surely you began to realize that values may have changed over time. Some values are constant throughout one's life. Others shift and assume less importance. Knowing one's values is key to setting goals and prioritizing one's needs.

In **Chapter 7**, "Time to Do Good…And for Good Times," you can take the opportunity to understand how you want to organize your **time** and your lifestyle. What are the opportunities and choices of more free time? Is your time unlimited? Do you want to **volunteer** in some meaningful organization? Is travel a significant part of your future? Do you have a hobby that deserves more time and attention from you? What about social activities? Are you interested in further schooling for fun or a degree? Retirees have often found "life-long learning" to be a very rewarding portion of their retirement plan. Is **leisure** on your list of priorities and how do you want to structure that leisure?

Once you have sorted out all your dreams, it's time to pull those all together and organize them into a viable plan. **Chapter 8**, "Your Action Plan," is designed to help you summarize your thoughts and ideas for the future and to create a solid action plan. Your plan is a **work in progress** and should be **reviewed at least annually** for desired changes and in line with new opportunities and new priorities. This action plan will form the structure for moving ahead. It doesn't mean that your plan will be cast in stone and never change. As we all know, we are always evolving and changing and those changes will affect the plan in the future. But for now it's important to put down some realistic goals for yourself and start on your journey. Remember what the Zen masters say: "A journey of a thousand miles begins with the first step." So, to get you ready for those first steps, you will fill out your action plan and put some time frames around the goals you have selected. The **Summary of Decisions** at the end of each chapter will help you create your action plan.

To assist you in creating your action plan, you might want to read some of the books in the bibliography, which is found at the end of the book. There are also many websites and on-line resources that can help you. You may want to refer to the book "Invent Your Retirement…Resources for the Good Life" by Art Koff. In his book, Mr. Koff not only identifies precisely how one accesses many on-line resources, but serves to identify other interesting topics that could not be fully covered in the 8 chapters previously discussed. For example, he lists cities where seniors tend to relocate; it covers the "Do not call" registry and how to deal with identity fraud; he recommends getting a pet (choosing a dog); as well as presents contact information for non-profits and charities and even discusses notes and poetry upon the passing of a friend. In other words, he presents lots of varied, interesting stuff!

Are you ready?

But, are you ready emotionally to consider retirement in the very near future? Does your projected image of retirement appear as a time for fulfillment, relaxation, growth, freedom, and renewal supported by friends and family? Or is retirement going to be a time you will need to formulate a way to deal with unstructured time, with your identity, with job loss, with re-creating relationships, and so forth. These two pictures are vastly different.

 To help you determine where you are in the emotional change process, please turn to **Exercise 3 (page 22),** "Self-Exploration: Are You Truly Emotionally Really Ready to Consider Retirement Soon?" When you will have finished this exercise you can determine where you stand on this spectrum of emotional readiness.

What did you learn about your readiness for retirement? Are there some challenges in your ability to retire emotionally? How difficult will it be for you to overcome these challenges?

If you feel ready and are wondering what to do next, think about this. As a retiree you will now have more time to engage in solving some of society's problems. Based on the activities in **"Customize Your Retirement."**© you will begin to get more closely in touch with your talents and interests and learn ways to apply those to cultural and societal changes that you want to impact. Retirees these days are not only living longer, but they are in better health, have more extensive educational backgrounds and have more skills than previous generations. Focusing your energy on problems that society faces may inspire you to bring about needed change and, at the same time, bring you personal gratification. Investigate **Chapter 7** "Time to Do Good…and For Good Times" to evaluate your interests and where and how you would like to spend your time.

And, then too, a large percentage of the retiring population wants to continue working for pay. Many will not have saved enough to retire completely; others feel the need to continue their careers; and others want the more tangible feedback that comes with monetary remuneration. For a great many, though, there is a need for change in their work life. People want more flexibility in their schedules, whether that means part-time rather than full-time work; more balance between work and leisure so that there is time to spend with family and friends; more time for travel and so forth. Others may want to change careers completely and follow a dream from the past. Still others may want to pursue more schooling, whether that is for a degree or simply to develop new skills or gather more information on a favorite subject. When you start planning your retirement you will begin to uncover some of these options and start to make choices.

You may be interested in reading through **Chapter 6** "Work is No Longer Work" to ponder your strengths, experiences and need for working. What are your interests? What are your hobbies? What are you willing to change in your life and what are you willing to risk? Take the time now to dream and create a vision for yourself of an ideal job. Don't rule out anything. Make a list of the various positions/jobs you have held in the past or are currently holding. Under each position, list three things about that job that you enjoyed most and when you felt most personally satisfied. Next, make a list of how you spend your discretionary income because that can be a good indicator of your priorities. Finally, look back over your life and think about all the dreams and ambitions that might have gotten sidetracked by practical concerns, such as financial security to pay the mortgage or put your kids through college. These lists can help you design a new career and help you find and follow your dreams.

So, how adaptive, flexible and versatile are you really? Many self-evaluation instruments and research studies have been created over the years to confirm the attributes needed by individuals to assist them in dealing with changing life and environmental conditions. Moving into retirement represents change, and it should be evident that it takes a certain temperament, a set of skills, plus a plan to successfully deal with this transition. As in all career transitions, and certainly a person's move into retirement represents a career change or transition, or perhaps even more than that…a transformation of sorts requires skill and planning.

 So what are you to make of this? Are you ready for change? Please turn to **Exercise 4 (page 24)**, "How Adaptive, Flexible, and Versatile Are You Really?" which will get you started thinking about yourself in transition.

What did you learn about yourself from this exercise? We all think we're very flexible until we begin to analyze the choices we have made in the past. Change and transition will be inevitable in planning the next phase of your life and being flexible is a key ingredient. Let's now look into how retirement itself has changed in the recent past.

This era is often referred to as the "New Retirement." What does that mean? It means that retirement for this new aging population will be different than it was for previous generations. Retirement no longer means "pulling back," as the word implies. It really means **moving forward** and that's why it is so often labeled differently. Some of the more popular labels and book titles are "Prime Time," "Don't Retire—Rewire," "The Third Age," "The Second Half," etc.

The new ideal retirement is a balance between an opportunity to derive pleasure, and, at the same time, having a sense of achievement. Working, volunteering and creating something new are all avenues to feeling fulfilled. So for you who may be thinking that retirement will be a week of Sundays, "I can play golf every day," others may be frightened by all that free time—lack of structure, lack of identity (who am I now?). And still others may feel that they must work. You might be missing your pals from work and haven't made friendships outside of work. No matter which way you go, change will impinge on your lifestyle. Change always involves losing something and gaining something. There are very few role models for retiring successfully. Our parents typically didn't have a very rewarding retirement. Perhaps they took a few trips, but were then overwhelmed by ill health and only found stimulation in front of the TV. Who are your role models? There are a lot of questions about retirement and there aren't many travel guides or road maps to tell you which way to go.

"Customize Your Retirement."© was designed to act as a **road map** and **travel guide** to help you plan your personal retirement. Take your time. This is an opportunity to "kick back" and dream a little, to listen to those inner voices and begin to respond to your dreams. This is a time for **building possibilities**, for **imagining changes** and for **making choices**.

Transition:

Everyone contemplating retirement envisions that there will be changes that need to be considered. Some people are very concerned about change, even though, if you look back on your life, change has been a constant. Some were positive and others negative, but all of them required a period of adjustment. Every transition involves leaving behind a known situation and moving into a relatively unknown situation. William Bridges, in his work on transitions, notes that there are 3 stages of change: there is an "ending phase," a "transition phase" and a "new beginning phase." In the "ending phase," there are losses, such as friendships that fade, status, identity and so forth. In the "transition phase," one is in neutral, exploring possibilities and figuring out what to do next. Finally, the "new beginning phase" develops in which a new identity is built and a new life is created. These phases or stages are not distinct, but overlap and frequently one bounces back and forth between them.

 It is obvious that you have weathered many changes and transitions in your life. To help you remember these "Chapters in Your Life" we have created **Exercise 5 (page 27)**. Take at look at this one and enjoy remembering the key events in your life. What did you find were your most important chapters? Did they involve luck, a focus on planning and persistence or just "drifting" through life? You may be astounded at how well you have structured your life and the fact that things didn't happen accidentally. These memories can help forge a new chapter in your life, your retirement.

As we begin to formulate a new chapter in our lives, it helps to remember:

> **"Age is opportunity no less**
> **Than youth, though in another dress.**
> **And as the evening twilight falls away**
> **The sky is filled with stars, invisible by day."**
> H.W. Longfellow, *Morituri Salutamus*
> (1807-1882)

If one can accept the transition to age, that is the first step. One must begin to reorient oneself to age. You will find yourself renewed when you embrace the reality; it becomes a source of strength. You are then able to take that next step in your life development.

Each of us lives a life that we believe has meaning for ourselves, for those we love and value and perhaps, for the community at large. In **Exercise 6 (page 28)**, "How Do You Define 'Life's Meaning' for Yourself," you will begin to ask yourself some questions about your life and what opportunities still await.

In completing that exercise, you may now have a taste for what might be in store for you in the coming years. At this point it may be helpful to understand the emotional ups and downs inherent in creating a "new beginning."

As you search for your vision, you may experience a flatness and emptiness or meaninglessness which is often the sign that you are in the transition/neutral phase. As Carl Jung, the 20th century Swiss psychiatrist, cautioned, "We cannot live the afternoon of life according to the programme of life's morning." So this is an opportunity to step back at midlife; to re-appraise and re-orient. This is a time to prepare for our coming life and its demands. This is a time to search for role models; to search within ourselves for how we wish to spend the coming precious years.

In reflecting upon life, many individuals dwell on "what might have been," or decisions they wish they had not made or unplanned circumstances that occurred causing them considerable unhappiness. It is easy to get into this "negative" mind game.

It is better by far to concentrate on one's successes in life, i.e. times that brought you happiness, pride, a sense of accomplishment, recognition, monetary reward, and so forth. It is said that success in life is partially luck and circumstance, but more important is the ability to create circumstances, develop skills, knowledge, and contacts as well as the attitude that fosters success.

It is exciting to reflect on one's successes and contemplate more future successes. As we continue down that road, we can add specific achievements and more details to our past successes and achievements.

 As we go through life, each of us has times of achievement, and days when time passes without notice as we simply manage our lives. In reflecting on these events in our lives, please turn to **Exercise 7 (page 29)**, "Perceived Life Satisfaction" and spend a few minutes remembering past achievements and contemplating new dreams to be lived.

Looking at our achievements and successes and looking for patterns allows us to contemplate future successes and achievements and more accomplishments to come. The transition into retirement can be full of joy and not as fearful as one might imagine.

In summary, retirement is a journey worth taking. With the help of **"Customize Your Retirement."**© you can plan for the retirement you've always wanted. First is to decide where you want to go, because every trip needs a destination. Then you need to understand how to pay for this trip. Getting your vehicle ready for the long haul is also important. What kind of vehicle will you need for this journey? Who will be going with you? Will you be taking side trips and enjoying the view or are you only focused on the destination? What will be different about this trip and what changes will you need to make to get ready? Do you need help in organizing yourself for your journey? Can you be specific about your plan?

Your future is coming fast. Plan for it so you can enjoy it!

 There are numerous individuals who can assist you or clarify matters relating to better planning for your retirement. Turn to **Exercise 8 (page 30)**, "Whom to Talk To in Making Plans for the Future," to get you started on creating a list of those people you want to talk to when making your plans for your retirement.

We thank you for being interested enough in your future to want to start planning for it. So get out there and start your journey. No regrets; no looking back; just building your dreams for this next exciting phase of your life.

 For even more help and experienced people to talk to who are trained in retirement planning, please call the **RetireRight Center** for an appointment to meet with someone, either on the phone or in person. **312-673-3842 or** www.retirerightcenter.org

TIPS

CHAPTER 1

PATH 1: ENVISION YOUR IDEAL RETIREMENT

EXERCISES

If you have not already done so, now is your opportunity to complete the following exercises which will assist you in examining your vision or dreams about retirement, thereby, hopefully, helping you to consider dealing with alternative solutions and opportunities.

Exercise 1: Introducing "Customize Your Retirement"©

Exercise 2: Your Values Clarification Opportunity

Exercise 3: Are you Emotionally Ready?

Exercise 4: How Adaptive, Flexible and Versatile Are You Really?

Exercise 5: The Chapters of Your Life

Exercise 6: How Do You Define "Life's Meaning" for Yourself?

Exercise 7: Perceived Life Satisfaction

Exercise 8: Whom to Talk to in Making Plans for the Future

At the conclusion of the exercises is a "**Summary of Decisions**" page, which will allow you to think through some of the thoughts and ideas you have been gathering in completing this chapter. Please take some time to evaluate the information you have both reviewed and created, and then summarize in writing some key points that you would like to pursue in putting together your final action plan in this book's last chapter, "**Your Action Plan…Putting It All Together**".

EXERCISE 1

INTRODUCING "CUSTOMIZE YOUR RETIREMENT"©

How clear are you about your retirement goals?

1. I know clearly what is important to me in my retirement years.   Yes ___ No ___
2. I am aware of my values and preferences and their impact on
        my retirement plans.   Yes ___ No ___
3. I know specifically what types of work or leisure activities I
        like best and how I want to use my time in retirement.   Yes ___ No ___
4. I can list my strongest skills and interests and how I want to
        apply those in the coming years.   Yes ___ No ___
5. I can list and define areas of interest or opportunity that I want
        to pursue in planning my retirement.   Yes ___ No ___
6. I am clear about my psychological readiness for retirement.   Yes ___ No ___
7. I am aware of my financial position and how it will impact my
        retirement.   Yes ___ No ___
8. I have worked with a financial planner to set financial goals.   Yes ___ No ___
9. I am saving appropriately for my retirement.   Yes ___ No ___
10. I have discussed our financial future with my spouse or
        significant other and we are in agreement with our plans.   Yes ___ No ___
11. I am pursuing ideas to identify sources of future income.   Yes ___ No ___
12. I know what vital papers and forms I need to complete, such as
        a will, estate plan, living will, etc.   Yes ___ No ___
13. I am aware of how my current lifestyle affects my health.   Yes ___ No ___
14. I am doing what is necessary to maintain my health and fitness.   Yes ___ No ___
15. I know what the stressors are in my life and know how to cope
        with them.   Yes ___ No ___
16. I have check-ups on a regular basis.   Yes ___ No ___
17. I have thought about how I will cope with illness in myself or a
        close family member and have planned how to address this issue. Yes ___ No ___
18. My current housing situation is ideal for my retirement years.   Yes ___ No ___
19. I have a specific plan for why and how I will relocate or change
        my housing to better respond to my retirement needs.   Yes ___ No ___
20. I have made arrangements to be near to my most important
        relatives (including children and grandchildren) in the coming years. Yes ___ No ___
21. My housing can accommodate my future health and exercise needs. Yes ___ No ___
22. I have fully researched and planned out where I want to live in
        retirement.   Yes ___ No ___
23. I am/will be comfortable with my "new identity" as a retired person. Yes ___ No ___
24. I am comfortable in projecting that my new roles in retirement will
        positively impact my "sense of self."   Yes ___ No ___
25. I am comfortable with the relationships I have with family and
        friends.   Yes ___ No ___

26. My relationships with family and friends will be a source of
    contentment and stability as I move into my retirement years.   Yes ___ No ___
27. I have a plan for action if I want or need to work in my
    retirement years.   Yes ___ No ___
28. I know how I will find contentment or fulfillment or how I will
    fulfill a passion in my work when I retire.   Yes ___ No ___
29. I have a plan for how I will work a different schedule than I do
    now, (i.e. perhaps either part-time or seasonally.)   Yes ___ No ___
30. I know how to transition into a new field.   Yes ___ No ___
31. I know how to market myself to find a new job.   Yes ___ No ___
32. I have planned how I will use my time in my retirement years.   Yes ___ No ___
33. I don't plan on being a volunteer or I envision doing volunteer
    work and have a plan for doing so.   Yes ___ No ___
34. In having an interest, I also have a plan for devoting more time
    to education and learning non-work related subjects in retirement.   Yes ___ No ___

Scoring:

I.   If you answered "no" to any question(s) **1-6,** refer to the **Envision Your Retirement**
     Chapter #1 of **"Customize Your Retirement"**© and take advantage of the exercises
     and ideas in that portion of the book.

II. If you answered "no" to any question(s) **7-12,** refer to the **Financial Picture** Chapter
     #2 and complete some of the exercises and begin to formulate plans for how to
     handle your finances with an eye to your retirement.

III. If you answered "no" to any question(s) **13-17,** refer to the **Getting in Shape** Chapter
     #3 and take advantage of the exercises offered and contemplate any changes you
     want to make in preparing your physical self for retirement.

Iς. If you answered "no" to any question(s) **18-22,** refer to the **Being at Home** Chapter
     #4 and begin to formulate ideas about housing needs in your retirement.

ς.   If you answered "no" to any question(s) **23-26,** refer to the **Vitalizing Relationships**
     Chapter #5, complete some of the exercises and begin contemplating how your
     relationships will be changing and how you will address these changes.

ςI. If you answered "no" to any question(s) **27-31,** refer to the **Work is No Longer
     Work** Chapter #6 and with the aid of the exercises presented, start formulating your
     career plans for the future.

ςII. If you answered "no" to any question(s) **32-34,** refer to **Time to Do Good and For
     Good Times** Chapter #7 where you will work through several exercises and become
     more focused on how you will be using your time in retirement.

If you answered "no" in all sections, just plunge in to any of the chapters and get started in
building your retirement plan. WAKE UP AND DREAM. Take charge of the rest of your
life.

[Please return to Page 9 to continue reading Chapter 1.]

EXERCISE 2
YOUR VALUES CLARIFICATION OPPORTUNITY

Our values are highly personal and develop throughout our lifetimes. They may vary, evolve or simply disappear as we move through our life stages. Now, as you are planning your retirement, is a good time to re-examine your values. Below is a list of common values. (A value is something that is important, desirable or useful to you as an individual in making decisions. It may vary over time and circumstance.) Please feel free to add to the list if something important is missing for you. Rate each value as **high/medium/low** so that you can ponder the relative importance of these values. Values are also important if you are planning to examine your career options to discover which values exist or don't in your current or planned work environment. When you reach the end of the list, please select the 3 to 6 values that you feel are most important to you at this point in your life.

Value	H	M	L	Value	H	M	L
Achievement				Education/Learning			
Altruism				Surroundings/Environment			
Creativity				Self-Fulfillment			
Financial security				Security			
Family				Helping others			
Recognition				Independence			
Friendships				Competition			
Change				Emotional well-being			
Freedom				Personal growth			
Leadership				Status			
Leisure time				Location			
Power				Philosophy/Religion			
Travel				Spirituality			
Risk-taking				Fun			
Caring				Adventure			
Prestige				Physical health			
Belonging				Emotional health			
Professionalism				Harmonious relations			
Control				Responsibility			

Please list below the values or conditions you care about most. Try to list them in order of priority, i.e., the ones you care about most should be 1 and 2, etc. These high priority values will be the ones that will "drive" your behaviors and actions in finding fulfillment in the next stage/phase of your life, your retirement.

1.	2.	3.
4.	5.	6.

[Please return to page 11 to continue reading Chapter 1]

EXERCISE 3

TIME TO DETERMINE WHETHER YOU ARE TRULY EMOTIONALLY REALLY READY TO CONSIDER RETIREMENT SOON?

Does your projected image of retirement appear as a time for fulfillment, relaxation, growth, freedom, and renewal supported by friends and family? Or, is retirement going to be a time of discomfort and of lack of direction; where job loss will put your identity in question, where newly acquired unstructured time could be seen as time that is squandered away, where relationships with others could become problematic, or where concerns about health become prominent causing your natural enthusiasm to slip away? These are two very different pictures; one of hope and renewal; the other of instability and concern. So where are you...confident, prepared and looking forward to the day when you enter a new career called "retirement", or one that reflects resistance or discomfort with that eventual occurrence?

To determine your emotional readiness, answer the following questions with a Yes or No answer. When you have finished answering the questions, you will have a better idea of where matters stand.

YES	NO	QUESTION
		1. Do I have sufficient interest in things to do to fill my hours and days in retirement?
		2. Will I be able to wake up in the morning excited about what I will do that day?
		3. Will I feel personal self-worth without the need to accomplish my work challenges?
		4. Will I feel personally okay without the identity of my job/occupation or title?
		5. Will my spouse, partner, or others close to me mind my being around more?
		6. Will my partner or significant others be comfortable without my income stream?
		7. Will I be free of financial worry in retirement?
		8. Do I have personal unfinished dreams, passions, or achievements outside of work yet to be fulfilled?
		9. Do I look forward to carefree days where I can do what I want?
		10. Do I consider myself sufficiently self-reliant to deal with changing future circumstances?
		11. Have I thought where I will live at the outset of retirement?
		12. Would my spouse, partner, or important family members be supportive my plans to retire?
		13. Would my friends be supportive of my plans to retire?
		14. Am I clear about my living standards in retirement?

YES	NO	
		15. Have I examined my monthly budget and expenditures sufficiently to know what I can afford in retirement and have I discussed this with my spouse, partner, or other important family members?
		16. Do I feel comfortable going to see a ballgame, movie, or other fun event in the middle of a weekday afternoon?
		17. Do I have family or friends whom I can spend more time with in the future?
		18. Will I be comfortable being at home while my spouse/partner continues working?
		19. Have I thought how I will handle family health and insurance needs initially upon entering retirement?
		20. Have I discussed how I will use my leisure time once retirement commences?
		21. Have I considered if I will be under financial pressure to earn money in retirement and, if so, have I planned for it?
		22. Have I planned what to say when others ask me to help them assuming I have time available to do so in retirement?
		23. Could I describe a typical day two years following onset of retirement?
		24. Do I picture a positive retirement experience for myself that I am prepared for?
		TOTAL SCORES

Interpretation of your Scores:

Scores of 22 to 24 "yes" answers: You are very well prepared to take the journey and enter a new phase in your life, or alternatively, you are misinterpreting your projections due to misreading of the questions or misunderstanding how matters will unfold. We hope you are well prepared, not misinformed.

Scores of 16 to 22 "yes" answers: You are well on your way in planning a successful transition and have a good sense for self and others. Continue on the track you are on. Perhaps spend more time with others ensuring they see the future as you do. Perhaps, also gain additional knowledge through reading, or by gaining advice and coaching from others who have managed a successful transition.

Scores of 10 to 15 "yes" answers: You are only half way there and need to reflect on what is getting in the way. Is it "too much on my plate now", a lack of support from others, fear of change and the future, or simply a belief that retirement is still too distant? If the prospect of retirement is not more than 5 years into the future, "Stop, Consider, and Discuss" this situation with others of importance. It has been said "Time waits for no man [woman]" and you need to build time for retirement planning into your schedule.

Scores below 10 "yes" answers: Review your "no" answers individually and begin to plan ahead. Seek help from others. Begin addressing matters now if you hope some day to retire with an element of happiness. Remember, an unplanned future is most often a future of chaos and disappointment.

[Please return to page 12 to continue reading Chapter 1.]

EXERCISE 4

HOW ADAPTIVE, FLEXIBLE AND VERSATILE ARE YOU REALLY?

First, assess your readiness for the change. Then, second, develop a plan which is the fundamental reason for this book.

Let's begin by having you complete the following exercise which we have adapted taking some of the considerations of adaptability, flexibility, and versatility derived from a study that was funded by the U.S. Army Research Institute for the Behavioral and Social Sciences, "The Application of a Model of Adaptive Performance to Army Leader Behaviors," May 2007. In their study, they found 8 attributes that individuals use to deal with changing life situations. They are listed below.

When thinking about dealing with change, particularly the transition into retirement, How Would You Describe Your Skills and Attitude in the following 8 Important Areas for Dealing with Change?

Taking Stock Quiz: My Resilience Quotient

How Would I Rate My Level of Capabilities, Skills and Attitudes in the Following 8 Important Competencies for Dealing with Change?

Competencies for Dealing with Change	Sample Skills and Attitudes	My Level of Competency Score: High = 5 Points Medium = 3 Points Low = 1 Point
1. Ability in handling emergencies	Skills: React quickly, maintain emotional control and objectivity and take action. Attitude: Understand urgent nature.	
2. Ability to handle daily stress	Skills: Effectively adjust plans, actions, goals, priorities to changing circumstances as needed, act professional with others. Attitude: Remain cool and do not over-react, manage my frustrations well.	

Competencies for Dealing with Change	Sample Skills and Attitudes	My Level of Competency Score: High = 5 Points Medium = 3 Points Low = 1 Point
3. Having problem-solving and creativity skills	Skills: Employ different analysis approaches and think outside given parameters, develop innovative methods, and find resources to accomplish solutions. Attitude: Being open-minded, resourceful, with a "can do" orientation.	
4. Effectiveness in dealing with unpredictable and changing situations	Skills: Readily and easily change gears, adjust and take action, structure responses in light of incomplete information. Attitude: Being flexible and refuse to be paralyzed by ambiguity.	
5. Learning new things…tasks, technology, ways of doing things	Skills: Do what is necessary to seek new knowledge and skills. Attitude: Be open-minded to learning.	
6. Demonstrating interpersonal adaptability	Skills: Develop effective relationships with others and demonstrate a keen insight into others' behavior and adjust accordingly to persuade, influence, or work with others. Attitude: When dealing with others, listen to their viewpoints and opinions and alter opinion when appropriate; be open and accepting of negative or developmental feedback.	
7. Displaying cultural (environmental) adaptability	Skills: Take action to understand the orientation, needs, and values of others or the other aspects of environment in which one exists. Think about how opinions and actions will impact others. Attitude: Understand the implications of actions toward maintaining a positive impact on others.	

Competencies for Dealing with Change	Sample Skills and Attitudes	My Level of Competency Score: High = 5 Points Medium = 3 Points Low = 1 Point
8. Having physically-oriented adaptability	Skills: Take action to adjust to challenging environmental states such as extreme heat, dirtiness, etc. Attitude: Believe one can create a reasonable response to difficult circumstances.	
9. The ability to have insight into one's own reality	Skills: Be able to recognize one's own emotions and perceptions and how these impact others. Take personal accountability for one's reactions and decisions. Attitude: Emphasize appropriate boundaries in dealing with others.	
	Total Score:	

What Do My Scores Say About Me?

Total Score: A score of over 33 points indicates you have a **Very Good to Excellent** set of skills to respond to change. You are quite resourceful and resilient.

A score of 20 to 32 points indicates you have a **Solid or Good** facility to respond to change. You are reasonably able to deal with changing circumstances that could impact both positively and negatively. Examine what you can do to eliminate scores below 3.

A score of 19 or less suggests you should focus on your ability to cope with changing circumstances. You have a reasonably low resiliency or versatility score. Perhaps spending time observing those who do well in responding to change or adversity would demonstrate how you could improve your skills in the arena. Additionally, seek assistance from others to coach or counsel how you might further address these sets of skills. Remember, they are skills you can acquire if you choose to do so.

[Please return to page 13 to continue reading Chapter 1.]

EXERCISE 5

THE CHAPTERS OF YOUR LIFE

Imagine that you are writing your autobiography. Think over the key events in your life. These are your chapter headings. Take a few minutes, now, to write out the names of the chapters of your autobiography. Into what segments does your life naturally divide? Write down the phrases that capture what each of those divisions felt like to you.

1. Under each chapter heading, list the 3 things about that time in your life that you enjoyed. When making your list, don't rule out anything: jobs, school, volunteer, leisure, social, spiritual, friendships, etc.

2. You may notice 1 or 2 things that appear over and over in various chapters and descriptions. This can help you focus on what you really like to do.

3. Think about what motivated your interests to begin with and what parts you have most enjoyed.

4. Summarize by listing the major interests and activities that your list brought out.

NEXT:

Discuss your summarized list with a partner. Did you have any "aha's"? Any insights? Any insights you could use in planning your future, particularly in retirement?

[Please return to page 14 to continue reading Chapter 1.]

EXERCISE 6

HOW DO YOU DEFINE "LIFE'S MEANING" FOR YOURSELF?

Each of us lives a life that we believe has meaning for ourselves, for those we love and value and perhaps, for the community at large. Therefore, each of us hopefully lives our life in a way that adds value, and a life we can take comfort in saying, "My life has had meaning."

To examine one's life, it is appropriate to begin by looking at three elements:

1. Who am I as a person?

2. How have I impacted others?

3. How successful was I in achieving what I sought to accomplish?

Certainly, if one reflects on these matters, most of us probably see the current state of one's life as a mix of successes and perhaps, some misses or opportunities that were not fully used. Unless you want it to be, RETIREMENT IS NOT THE FINISH LINE for having achievements…MUCH MORE CAN YET BE ACCOMPLISHED AND IT IS IMPORTANT TO CONTINUE STRIVING TO LEAVE A MORE COMPLETE REPUTATION, LEGACY, ACCOMPLISHMENT OR TO ACHIEVE PERSONAL FULFILLMENT.

To expand my meaning in life:

What do I yet want TO DO?

What do I yet want TO BE?

What do I yet want TO HAVE?

[Please return to page 15 to continue reading Chapter 1.]

EXERCISE 7

PERCEIVED LIFE SATISFACTION

For future satisfactions, it is important to reflect on our significant achievements, regrets and passions from our previous years.

In the first column, please name the most important events in your life (either positive or negative.) Why are they important? List those reasons in the second column.

Most important:	Important because:

What are the really significant achievements you are proud of?

1. _____
2. _____
3. _____
4. _____
5. _____

To what extent do you have a remaining passion to do something, or an unfulfilled dream that needs to be completed or achieved? What would it be?

Or to what extent do you look upon your remaining years as an opportunity to gain greater fulfillment or enjoyment? How so? (Please indicate briefly below.) Do you see your remaining years as a time of principally managing day-to-day?

[Please return to page 15 to continue reading Chapter 1.]

29

EXERCISE 8

WHOM TO TALK TO IN MAKING PLANS FOR THE FUTURE

There are numerous individuals who can assist you or clarify matters relating to better planning for your retirement. The following is a starting list. Your individual situation could also identify other individuals that you may wish to add to this list.

<u>Whom To Speak To</u>	<u>About Which Subjects</u>	<u>How Soon?</u>
Spouse/Partner		
Accountant		
Investment Counselor		
Best Friends (List Names)		
Adult Children		
Siblings		
Parents		
Other Important Relatives		
Your Clergy		
One's Attorney		
Your Physicians • Generalist/Internist • Other key physicians		
Medicare & Social Security		
All Previous Employers (if entitled to Pensions)		

(This list continues on the next page.)

Whom To Speak To	**About Which Subjects**	**How Soon?**

Independent Living or
Other such Facilities

Your Union,
the Veteran's Administration,
or Professional Organizations
(if entitled to services
or future employment)

Residence/Community Leaders

Teacher/Instructor

Realtors

Paid Counselors
- Psychologist
- Psychiatrist
- Retirement Consultant
  - The RetireRight Center
    In Chicago

Funeral Homes & Cemeteries

Others to Gain Information or
Advice…Please Name Them Below
-
-
-
-

[Please return to page 16 to continue reading Chapter 1.]

SUMMARY OF DECISIONS

PATH 1: ENVISION YOUR IDEAL RETIREMENT

In this chapter, "**Envision Your Ideal Retirement,**" you have been introduced to the book, "Customize Your Retirement."© After having completed the exercises in this chapter, you should have reached some personal decisions which will later become **key (critical) inputs toward completing your final Action Plan in Chapter 8.** Think about what you would like **to do more of,** or perhaps, what you would like to **do less of** in preparing for your most realistic and fulfilling retirement. Consider in what capacity you see yourself changing your goals and actions in the future and why.

 You Decide

What do I want to commit to working on related to my vision of a successful retirement?

1.   I would like to work on developing my dreams for the future, and creating a vision of my ideal retirement.

2.   I would like to work on determining what some of the challenges and choices are that await me in the coming years.

3.   I would like to expand my knowledge drawn from the exercises in this booklet; for example: my emotional readiness, my flexibility, my life's successes, and so forth as they relate to planning retirement.

4.   I would like to work on discussing my dreams, challenges and choices for the future with those people who are important to me.

What are your **key decisions?**

Key Decision A

_____

_____

Key Decision B

_____

_____

Key Decision C

_____

_____

Other thoughts, questions, ideas, research that needs to be done, etc.

Please transfer your decisions into Chapter 8 (Page 226): "Your Action Plan."

CHAPTER 2

PATH 2: THE FINANCIAL PICTURE...MAKING IT A MASTERPIECE

"It is not how much one makes but to what purpose one spends."
John Ruskin (1819-1900) English art critic

In this chapter, you will have the opportunity to:

1. Explore the financial information that Boomers and others need to consider when transitioning into retirement.
2. Complete exercises that may help you to better understand your level of knowledge, your readiness and your comfort level relating to the various aspects of planning financially for your well-being in retirement.
3. Complete exercises to better understand what specific steps you have already taken and those that need to be taken to have a financially successful retirement.
4. Examine a special section following the exercises that attempts to identify alternatives for those believing they have insufficient money to live sufficiently in retirement.

What do you want out of your retirement?

Money matters. To do productive and creative thinking about your retirement and to realize your dreams, you need financial means and financial security.

To achieve personal fulfillment in the "new retirement," you need to know your present and future financial circumstances. You need to know your current and projected cash flow in order to plan for the lifestyle you want.

Your present living arrangements, whether it's a studio apartment or a 6000 square foot home, could change in the coming years. Your current financial situation could improve or deteriorate. Savings are critical to helping you deal with life's uncertainties. Then again, the lifestyle you choose may be comfortable for you, but merely barebones for someone else.

What has become evident in recent years is that social security will be insufficient to support most people's lifestyles. As well as the fear of social security diminishing, company defined pension plans are also quickly disappearing. Some of today's retirees have been fortunate in having pension plans made available to them and usually would be able to carry on a "traditional leisure lifestyle retirement."

Even employees at larger companies with traditional pension programs in place cannot assume that these programs will continue to exist for them. This possibility necessitates a need for people to plan for themselves and thus avoid being surprised later on if, like so many companies, their pensions become "frozen" or eliminated. According to the Employee Benefit Research Institute (EBRI) in the past two years, about a sixth of employees have seen a reduction in their retirement benefits. And, if you are not covered in or previously covered by a traditional defined pension plan, begin saving now on your own through a 401(K) or other savings plan because chances are you will not be entered into one in the future. Most plans "Grandfather" (cover) only those currently or previously entered into such a plan. There are many who are overconfident about these facts and think they will be covered when they will not be.

 It is interesting to note that about 60% of workers say that they expect to be covered by a defined benefit plan when in reality only about 40% say that they or their spouses currently have such a plan.
Consider This

Employee Benefit Research Institute (EBRI)

A June 6, 2006 article in the *Wall Street Journal* referred to the changes in retirement benefits as the disappearing "Golden Age of Retirement." Perhaps the model of previous generations having a carefree retirement has lulled Boomers into believing that this will also be available to them. What are your beliefs?

You are the lucky one. With the help of the materials in this book you will be better able to plan your retirement and make it what you would dream it to be.

**"Knowing is not enough; we must apply.
Willing is not enough; we must do".**
Johanne Wolfgang von Goethe (1749-1832), German poet, dramatist, novelist,
theorist, humanist, scientist, and painter

Do you believe that you will find fulfillment in the traditional leisure retirement lifestyle? Many people who attain this lifestyle report that it is not a satisfying outcome to their life's work. They don't feel stretched either intellectually or productively. In contrast, the current wave of retirees is seeking a new style of retirement, one that brings a new sense of mission, fulfillment and happiness.

Alternatives and the changing world of money for retirement

In today's world, there are an array of financial vehicles specifically designed for retirement funding; these vehicles include IRAs, Roth IRAs, SEP-IRAs, 403(b) plans for non-profits and 401(K)s for profit-making organizations, as well as retirement annuities and other instruments. The number of plan choices and flexibility toward establishing them is a growing phenomenon. The amount of money invested in these vehicles amounts to trillions of dollars.

Consider This

How do you make decisions with this dizzying array of choices? How comfortable are you in knowing about financial matters such as what investment vehicles to choose from? Do you consider yourself knowledgeable about how well Boomers in general are prepared for retirement? Do you know if you are better off than your colleagues in preparing for retirement and do you read up on current events affecting retirement planning?

To see how knowledgeable you are, you can take a brief exercise that follows in this chapter, **Exercise 1 (page 53),** "Self-testing: Your Knowledge About Financial Matters." If you choose to complete it, your answers will provide feedback on how well you are keeping abreast of matters in this pre-retirement planning arena. How did you score, and what implications are there for your future follow-up?

There are three major investment groups or classes. These are: (1) fixed investments, (2) equities and (3) bonds. Knowing how to divide up your savings via asset allocation is complex and critical to your financial security. The information in this chapter is not designed to replace your personal judgment in managing your money. If you feel insecure about making decisions on how to invest your money, it is strongly recommended you seek support from a "Certified Financial Consultant/Planner." These consultants have specialized knowledge and can map out the best ways for you to invest your funds.

"Money is like an arm or leg -- use it or lose it."
Henry Ford (1863-1947), American industrialist

Seeking professional help

There is a big need by Boomers to hire professional consulting to assist with planning financially for retirement. There appears to be some understanding of the need to do this, but the question of why professional advice is not followed is still a mystery.

About half of all workers say that they are likely to take advantage of and seek the advice of financial consultants, but only about 1 in 5 of these individuals say that they will implement all of the recommendations they receive.

Employee Benefit Research Institute (EBRI)

Is this non-compliance with professional recommendations due to the fact that the advice will be viewed as inappropriate for the individual, or too difficult to follow? Or is it viewed as too boilerplate and generic? Or is it based on the fact that insufficient information is shared or given truthfully to the consultant? Or the advice changed because of changing conditions or changing attitudes? Might there be other reasons? One can only speculate.

A word of caution: In *The CPA Journal, Online* (September 2005), the author Charlie Davidson, in an article entitled, "In the Service of Baby Boomers: A Seismic Mind Shift for Financial Service Providers" writes: 1. "Most advisors, although educated and intelligent, will be far removed from retirement and will not have experienced the need to distribute accumulated wealth"... 2. "The financial industry is largely centered on selling appropriate financial products and holding assets under management for as long as possible. This tactic will not work for Baby Boomers, who will consume their assets over time." ...3. The new focus will be on income for life and on products that facilitate careful and systematic **decumulation of a client's savings in retirement...i.e. phases-income and time-released cash flow strategies during retirement...**" This means finding a different type of financial consultant who will be able to advise you on how to release your money over time in order to have the best impact on your chosen lifestyle. This is important because at the beginning of one's retirement will be a time when the individual "will have the most money they will ever have and **new retirees will be forced to make almost instantaneous decisions about asset allocation, asset distribution, and product deployment, i.e. wealth distribution over time." The author advises: "This decumulation should be structured by a <u>formal written plan</u> recognizing the phases of retirement and unique needs and events that occur within those phases."**

It is critical that when you go to a professional for assistance, make sure beforehand that you and your spouse, partner or "significant other" are on the same page when it comes to a view of the future. Fidelity Investments surveyed people ages 43 to 70 and found that with more than 30% of the couples, the husband and wife gave completely different answers when asked when, where, and how they will retire.

TIPS

AARP The Magazine, July-August, 2007, "Avoid these Money Traps," Walecia Konrad.

In **Exercise 2 (page 55)**, "Determining How You Feel and Think about Your Financial Planning for Retirement", you are asked to examine for yourself how you think about your financial planning. Consider having your spouse, partner, or "significant other" also complete this exercise and compare your answers. What did you learn? Any surprises? What actions might your answers call for?

You
Decide

And since we are on the topic of written materials and plans, consider having a "health care directive" telling your doctor and family members what kind of care you would like if you are unable to make medical decisions. A "living will" becomes most important if you are terminally ill as it will instruct your loved ones how to proceed if you are unable to do so. Likewise a "health care power of attorney" will let someone else make medical decisions if you are too ill to make them. And, finally, a "Letter of Instructions" telling the location of your important papers (your will, military records, and birth and marriage certificates, a summary of your investments, the location of an inventory of your household possessions, the whereabouts of your safe deposit boxes, tax and gift returns, and funeral instructions and the names of those who should be notified upon your demise.) These are documents few like to contemplate, much less create, but you can understand how important they are.

Corporate responsibility for retirement planning

Pension plans are going the way of the Dodo Bird. Pension plans represent long term liabilities that senior management are often concerned about and think should be terminated because they are on their books and must be paid out many years into the future.

It appears that Corporations have also not really dealt with assisting individuals in planning for retirement. Human Resource organizations are often understaffed and focused on numerous other issues facing their organizations, such as: changes in organization strategy and tactics, compensation and union matters, succession planning, policy administration, payroll administration, recruiting and selection. Retirement planning is relegated to the "back burner." In fact, even if there were more attention paid to retirement planning, there is often a reluctance to provide in-company or company- sponsored professional advice for people on investment planning because of liability concerns. There is a universal "head in the sand" philosophy on the part of management and Human Resources that assumes that individuals are "adults" and therefore should deal with their own personal, private financial matters. [As an interesting side note, the most senior executives are often provided with financial consultants to advise them on their own portfolio management.]

Pensions…one check or many?

Did You Know?

"One Check or Many?" This is the title of a brief, but very informative article by Eric Tyson, author of the bestselling book Investing for Dummies, in the March & April 2007 issue of AARP Magazine. The article indicates that 7 out of 8 individuals take a monthly (annuity-like) payment rather than a lump sum payout in collecting their defined pension payouts. The article goes on to suggest that with Ford Motor Company and other companies having more financial difficulties, the decision to go this route of choosing a monthly pension payment may become a bit more difficult. The article provides a few suggested thoughts related to making the decision of one check or many. Here are a few of their suggestions:

- If family history or a medical problem leads a person to believe they may not have long to live, take the lump sum and invest it so it puts money immediately at the person's disposal, while allowing the remainder to go to their heirs.

- Many people take the money to dispose of debt, but this is suggested to be an avenue of last resort. The article suggests that the individual become disciplined in paying down their debts on a schedule and not use their pension money, and goes on to say that one should never use it to pay off a mortgage…Better, it suggests, to move into more affordable housing.

- Taking the advice of a financial consultant who states that they can get a better return than the pension monthly payout means you run the risk of losses and smaller payments as stock markets and other investments fluctuate over time.

Did You Know?

- Finally, if the worst were to happen and your company were to go bankrupt, the US Government's agency would in part pick up the obligation of monthly payments. For all but highly paid employees, the coverage should be fine. To determine if that is true for you, go to their site and determine what your government agency payout would be should the situation arise (www.pbgc.gov, click on "Workers and Retirees", then on "Maximum monthly guarantee tables.")

Pensions lost, perhaps not forever

The United States, from time-to-time, has taken steps to support individuals in their attempt to secure monies for their retirement. As described by EBRI (Employee Benefit Research Institute) in their "*Notes*" newsletter, Vol. 24, No. 12, December 2003, and their February, 2005 "*Facts from EBRI*" publication, a brief summary of legislation affecting vast numbers of employees includes:

- The Employee Retirement Income Security Act (ERISA) of 1978 was enacted to ensure that employees receive a pension and other benefits promised by their employers. ERISA has been modified over the years to incorporate and tie in the Internal Revenue Code provisions design so as to encourage employers to provide retirement and other benefits to their employees. These laws have been liberalized to encourage savings while still attempting to ensure that tax-favored pension plans do not favor the highest-paid employees over rank and file employees. Essentially, ERISA has created a single federal standard for employee benefits, and supersedes almost all state laws that affect employee benefit plans.

- Initially, a 401(k) provision of the 1978 Tax Revenue Act went largely unnoticed for two years. Ted Benna, a Pennsylvania benefits consultant, analyzed the law and devised a creative and rewarding application of the law. The 401(k) provision Section stipulated that cash or deferred-bonus plans qualified for tax deferral. Benna noticed that the clause did not preclude pre-tax salary reduction programs, contrary to the assumptions that contributions to such plans could be made only after income tax was withheld, a belief held by most other observers of tax law at the time. Benna researched the tax act and came up with his innovative interpretation of the 401(k) provision in 1980 in response to a client's proposal to transfer a cash-bonus plan to a tax-deferred profit-sharing plan.

- Fortunately, Ronald Reagan, in his campaign for the Presidency made personal saving through tax-deferred individual retirement accounts, or IRAs, a component of his campaign. Payroll deductions for IRAs were allowed in 1981. Benna hoped to extend that feature to his new plan. He established a salary-reducing 401(k) plan even before the Internal Revenue Service had finished writing the regulations that would govern it. The IRS surprised many observers when it provisionally approved the plan in Spring 1981 and specifically sanctioned Benna's interpretation of the law that fall. Benna's breakthrough earned him the appellation "the grandfather of 401(k)'s."

- From 1981 onward, 401(k) plans have quickly become a leading method of savings in the evolving retirement benefits business. The number of plans has increased more than 150 percent, and the rate of participation grew from less than 2/3 to 3/4 of all employees from 1984 to 1992. The number of employees participating in 401(k) plans rose to more than 19 million by 1991. This growth continued in the 1980s because individuals and the government realized the volume of salary reductions were in the employees' interest, but not in the government's best interest because of lost tax revenues. In fact, in 1986, the Reagan administration changed its support of these programs and made two attempts to invalidate 401(k)s in 1986—but public outrage prevented the attempt to quash the tax benefit revolution and the repeals failed.

- In 1996, legislation was initiated to expand the use of "hardship distribution rules" in companies with 100 or fewer employees so that individuals in those organizations could make hardship withdrawals from their 401(k) plans more easily. Also, in 1996, new legislation provided methods permitting employees to participate in a 401(k) plan before completing a year of service with an organization and allowed newly eligible employees to become automatically enrolled in their retirement savings plans, even if they take no action to enroll.

- The Pension Protection Act of 2006 expanded the role of the Pension Benefit Guaranty Corporation, a federal agency that insures most traditional pensions. The legislation also:

  o Ensures workers have additional information about their accounts' performance;
  o Provides for greater access to professional advice about investing for retirement;
  o Gives workers greater control over how their accounts are invested;
  o Makes permanent the higher contribution limits for IRAs and 401(k)'s that were passed in 2001, enabling more workers to build larger retirement nest eggs.
  o Requires companies that terminate their pension plans to provide extra funding for the pension insurance system;
  o Extends requirements on companies to measure their pension plan obligations more accurately;
  o Closes loopholes that allowed under-funded plans to skip pension payments;
  o Requires companies that under-fund their pension plans to pay additional premiums;
  o Raises caps on the amount that employers can put into their pension plans, so they can add more money during good times and build a cushion that can keep their pensions solvent in lean times;
  o Prevents companies with under-funded pension plans from digging the hole deeper by promising extra benefits to their workers without paying for those promises up front; businesses that offer a private pension plan to their employees have a duty to set aside enough money now, so their workers get what they have been promised when they retire.
  o The legislation removes barriers that prevent companies from automatically enrolling their employees in defined contribution plans.

Rules of thumb

There are many rules of thumb out there relating to retirement, but the one most quoted is that a person needs to calculate the "three legs of the stool"…i.e. their retirement income stream from 1. Social Security, 2. pensions, and 3. personal savings. Then they need to calculate their retirement outflow.

Rule of Thumb Typically, financial consultants advise you to calculate that you will need 70% of your annual pre-retirement income when you stop working, assuming you paid off your mortgage, and will have excellent health. If not, or if you want to travel often or go out to dinner often, and so forth, assume you will need a higher percentage…say 85% or more.

Keeping life simple is often thought to be the best route to success, which means having fewer possessions; having more cars or houses clearly requires more complexity and more money. As indicated above, if a person lacks a pension, then they need to fund more for retirement themselves. **Another rule of thumb**…Count on needing at least $10 to $15 in investment savings to cover each dollar that is not available from a pension (i.e. an income stream shortfall.) So, imagine that short fall to be $40,000. In that case a person needs a nest egg of at least $450,000 to as much as $600,000 in savings to bridge the gap. Typically, there are no shortcuts to amassing this amount of money…another simple rule applies and that is **one must save**.

RULE OF THUMB: **"Time is neutral"** which means that with time no problem ever gets solved. This means wise use of time beginning with a plan and a commitment to save can get you the money needed for retirement and the best time to start is as soon as possible.

Have you ever heard of a Monte Carlo calculator? It is a simulation that can be run by a financial advisor. Using a computer and various assumptions about how you apportion your savings portfolio, it can tell you how many years (or to what age) your money will last for you. Remember again that inflation will likely always continue to nibble away at what you get. As you spend your savings over time…rising inflation translates into a rising cost of living. How much for example will a person lose in purchasing power over 20 years with a 2.5% annual inflation rate: 40%!

Using Housing to Fund Retirement: Many individuals have a very high percentage of their net worth tied up in real estate, in some cases in excess of 60%. Unfortunately, in recent years individuals have been siphoning off equity in their homes as "piggy banks" spending these former savings for other uses. The result is increased mortgage debt. The philosophy behind this had been that house values appreciate. Unfortunately, as we have recently witnessed, housing can depreciate, and with it, the loss of a corresponding percent of net worth. Financial magazines suggest Boomers and others should put savings in their 401(k) and other savings accounts and not overextend on housing; housing in the future may well not fund retirement, especially the case for older Boomers.

GENERAL RULE OF THUMB among financial consultants is that a household should not: a) take on **total debt** in excess of about <u>a third of total household income</u> and should not b) take on **mortgage debt** of more than about <u>a quarter of total household income.</u>

Professional financial consultants advise that a person examine how they are tracking their money at least once a year. This is a suggestion, not a rule of thumb.
We all know the "The Savings Catch-up Game" is not an easy one to play if you are behind in getting your savings to the point needed. One universal rule applies among financial consultants…Don't panic, but also don't procrastinate…they all advise…act now for a better future.

To work or not to work. That is the question.

Today's retirees often need to find additional income to support their intended lifestyle. Even so, it is interesting to note that most "traditional" retirees work "to keep active," according to a Cornell Retirement and Wellbeing study. The need to earn additional income comes in a surprising fourth in a list of reasons that prompt retirees to return to work. Research confirms that often retirees return to work months, often several years after retirement, because of a lack of stimulation, challenge, the need to develop new relationships, or to obtain a sense of value.

Today's Boomers and other pre-retirees report that more than two-thirds of them are planning to work. Add to this number, those planning to perform non-paid voluntary services and you have a huge number of retirees planning to support organizations and/or individuals. Future retirees plan to combine work and volunteerism and see that as their dream retirement. This dream retirement will have them work toward fulfilling a life's mission or ambition. The work performed at this retirement stage is a way to use their life's experience, often life's tough lessons, toward the betterment of others. Jeri Sedlar and Rick Miners refer to this process in their book, "*Don't Retire, Rewire,*" as does Richard P. Johnson, PhD, in his book, *The New Retirement*.

Almost half of retirees work on a full or part-time basis. Although seeking additional income is not the primary motive to return to work, gaining "pocket change," secondary funds or medical and other benefits is enticing to "traditional leisure-style" retirees. For some obviously, not having sufficient funds to carry them through their retirement is a reality and they must work. An article in the *Wall Street Journal* from June 6, 2006 suggests that Generation X'ers (those born between 1965 and 1978) will not reach the level of savings to replace the future reduction or elimination of Social Security and defined benefits payments unless they dramatically begin to increase their level of savings. This could also be true for Boomers who have not saved sufficiently for their future years.

? Did You Know? According to a Fidelity Investment study on savings, some 15% of American families are on track to replace 85% of their pre-retirement income (their "Magic" target figure), and only 29% are on track to replace at least 70%. If you believe you also are short of your goals, be sure to **read the special section** following the exercises in this chapter entitled, "For Those Believing They Have Insufficient Money to Live Sufficiently in Retirement."

According to the Department of Labor, the fastest growing population of temporary and part-time workers is comprised of professionals. Kiplinger Magazine as far back as several years ago (March 2003) in an article called, " Will This Be Your Next Job...temporary work lets you be a free agent without running a business" suggested that temping could well be your next job, offering good benefits to those filling those positions. Will this be you in retirement?

Predicting your future retirement cash flow needs

As indicated earlier, typically, financial consultants state that to maintain your standard of living will require having at least 70-85% of your pre-retirement income.

To get a sense for the numbers, it is often stated by financial consultants that if a couple were to cap their withdrawals from their savings/portfolios to 4% per year, increasing that initial amount by the additional percent based on the annual rise in the cost of living identified by the US Government, then their savings should last throughout their retirement years. If they were to withdraw funds at the rate of 7% per year, their nest egg could perhaps last 30 years assuming no catastrophic event occurs in their lives. From a different perspective, a half million dollar nest egg could generate approximately $25,000-$30,000 per year in available funds over a retiree's lifetime. Indeed, you can see considerable savings are needed to live worry free. Most financial consultants can generate various withdrawal scenarios for you. You can also pursue this effort yourself by going to a number generator. A very good first resource is to read the book, *The Savage Number,* by Terry Savage.

> **RULE OF THUMB: "How long will my money last?"**
> Withdrawing at the rate of 10% year, it will only last about 11-12 years;
> Withdrawing 7% could provide funds for 17-18 years;
> Withdrawing 4% per year, the money should last essentially for life (well over three decades) which is the reason financial consultants advise limiting withdrawals to 4% per year, (adding a dollar amount reflective of the rate of inflation) to enhance the chances of having investment income for life.

You Decide

As a starting point, examine your future cash-flow needs by reviewing the following questions:

- How much will I need?
- Can I pay for my standard of living expenses without taking early withdrawals from retirement assets?
- Once retired, how much can I withdraw each year taking into account price inflation?
- How will I pay for health coverage at a level I will need?
- Do I have ways to make money if there is a shortfall?

Risk factors worth considering

Do not be conned into thinking that preparation for retirement is simply a matter of financial planning. It is clearly more (as you will discover in working through this book.) It is also a matter of circumstances. For example, no one can be totally accurate in forecasting the future. There are two unpredictable factors that are economy-driven and even the most knowledgeable financial consultants and gurus cannot predict:

a) "Return risk": The predicted rate of return on your investments over an extended period of time. (As those in the business of investing are quick to point out, "Past performance is no guarantee of future returns.")

b) "Inflation risk": The inflation rate over the long-term.

Nevertheless, planning is required for increasing your probability of financial security. Some of the steps needed to do this planning involve:

a) Knowing your spending habits and budgets.

b) Projecting a lifestyle in retirement and understanding *roughly* in today's dollars what it will take to fund your desired level of lifestyle.

c) Taking account of and making judgments on three personal wild cards affecting how much you will have over time:

You Decide

- "Your Mortality risk"= How long will you live?
- At what rate will you spend your money, i.e. the cash flow and the depletion of savings?
- To what extent should you account for unplanned events such as outlays upon deterioration of health, major catastrophic home repairs, the need to support adult children or other family members, or others in need, i.e. "Your Liability risk?"

d) Examining the dollars needed in retirement for b and c above and creating a savings plan that will move you towards your dream.

We have added a unique bingo-like exercise, **Exercise 3 (page 57),** "Financial PEACE" Exercise... **"PEACE = Ponder Everything And Check Essentials (for a Better Planned Tomorrow)."** This exercise is designed to help you determine the amount of planning, and more importantly, the actions you have to take in preparing adequately to protect yourself today, in the near future, and in your retirement years. You will examine if you have either completed the actions associated with each item, as described in the exercise, or minimally examined the item or specifically chosen not to do it because not doing it was in your best long-term interest. After completing the exercise, only you will know if you are preparing yourself for your future and that of your loved ones. We hope you do well in this exercise.

In the May/June 2007 issue of <u>Priority Magazine</u> titled, "Retire Right", the author Michaela Cavellaro provides an example of what you will have to save to get the cash flow needed in retirement. To illustrate, she uses $25,000 as needed annually to supplement Social Security, traditional pensions, and other income sources:

To generate a $25,000 annual return or income stream, one would need to accumulate a savings of $500,000 paid out at a 5% annual return. Putting $4,000 per year into an investment returning a high 8% return would net $485,383 after 30 years, close to the $500,000 needed to do this. Wait five years to start putting money aside and the accumulated gross return would end up at only $315,817, a far cry from the needed $500,000.

Consider This

The numbers above send a clear message: start saving as much as possible and as soon as possible. To learn more about dollars needed for retirement, find a retirement calculator. There are many out there to assist you in determining savings, portfolios, and retirement cash flows. You can "Google" retirement calculators and they will be identified for you. Once you have a calculator, enter in various assumptions and facts, and the calculators will provide numbers that you should evaluate to determine future savings.

On the other hand, most everyone has some level of disposable income. Few individuals spend their entire income stream on necessities, i.e. food, housing, utilities, medications, transportation, taxes, and the like. Not to say that there aren't folks that find themselves living in such conditions (hand-to-mouth).

Assuming that you have some level of disposable income, where do you plan to spend it, if not for saving for retirement? **Exercise 4 (page 60),** "Beyond Necessities: How You Plan to Spend Your Savings" provides an opportunity for you to further examine your choices.

If you completed Exercise 4, what did you discover? Were there items that really needed to be attended to, or was some money earmarked there simply for fun?

 If you are concerned that you will have a serious savings shortfall, be sure to **read the special section** following the exercises in this chapter entitled, "For Those Believing They Have Insufficient Money to Live Sufficiently in Retirement." **TIPS (page 61.)**

Interesting Long Term Care Insurance facts

Many workers assume they have the coverage, probably through Medicare, Medicaid or other insurance coverage, when in fact this support will not be there for them when the need arises. Make sure you have coverage for emergency health care and long-term care. Remember that this care may be needed well before retirement; accidents happen and younger individuals do fall victim to Alzheimer's disease, strokes, heart attacks, and so forth.

 According to the Employee Benefit Research Institute (EBRI) estimates, a full quarter of all workers and a third of retirees report having Long Term Care insurance to pay for nursing home, assisted living facility or in-home care, <u>but</u> **Did You Know?** only 10% of Americans actually have Long Term Care insurance coverage.

Most people think "nursing home" when they say Long Term Care insurance. But Long Term Care insurance also covers care you receive at home. The fact is, of the 12 million people receiving Long Term Care insurance coverage, only 1.5 million are in nursing homes.

Long term care actually refers to a wide range of services provided to those with a chronic illness or disability. At its core, it involves assistance with the most basic and personal activities of daily life; getting out of bed, getting dressed, going to the bathroom, etc. However, it can also include help with secondary tasks such as assistance with cooking and cleaning. "Long term care differs from other types of health care in that the goal of long term care is not to cure an illness, but to allow an individual to attain and maintain an optimal level of functioning." (U.S. Senate Special Committee on Aging, February, 2000.)

The second misconception about long term care is that it is something that happens only when you're old. Given that one study showed that Boomers defined "old age" as over 85, while the average life expectancy is 82, one can conclude that most Boomers really are still thinking that they will die before they get old. However, people can become incapacitated due to injury or illness at any age. Think of Michael J. Fox and Christopher Reeve. The fact is, over 37% of those receiving Long Term Care insurance coverage are under 65 years of age.

Annuities can provide retirement income streams

The purpose of an annuity is to convert your savings into a supplemental monthly income stream to augment Social Security, company pensions, work, and other sources of income that will provide the means for paying bills in retirement. There are many combinations and choices of annuity types in the marketplace and the choices continue to grow to include programs focused on medical health coverage. One can reduce all the choices to 4 basic combinations:

1. There is the "Fixed Annuity" which gives the recipient the same fixed amount over the length of the program.
2. Alternatively, one can choose a "Variable Annuity" that provides varying amounts over the pay-back period dependent on investment returns.
3. Typically individuals who request an immediate payout as an income stream will purchase an "Income Annuity."
4. However, a purchaser can hold off receiving a payout for a specified period in the future by buying a "Deferred Annuity."

Taking these 4 choices above in combination, one can purchase:

1. A Fixed Income annuity provides a fixed amount over a set period of time which can be a purchaser's entire life.

2. A Variable Income annuity offers variable payout amounts over an extended period (which can be a purchaser's entire life) based on investment results.
3. A Variable Deferred annuity provides variable amounts as payouts over a set period of time based on investment results which the recipient receives at some pre-determined future period.
4. A Fixed Deferred annuity offers further accumulated value at a pre-determined interest rate.

TIPS The sale of annuities is a competitive business and agents will compete for your business. Beyond the choices above, you will discover many programs that offer new incentives to make you, the buyer, interested in their "unique program." Be sure to evaluate each choice carefully on its own merit and then compare it to competitive products. If it seems very confusing or too good to believe (based on fancy fliers and quick-tongued brokers or agents), the best advice one can give is for you to refrain from buying until program choices are reviewed with an independent financial consultant. Often, you can do as well learning to invest or working with your financial consultant to create alternative income streams (for example, laddering CDs or treasury bonds) versus purchasing annuities for retirement years.

A final word about the variability of annuity payments; they can change over time tied to interest rates. Higher national interest rates result in higher variable annuity payments.

Did You Know? For example, a couple aged 65 purchasing an immediate annuity for $100,000 in May of a particular year would have received the following: In 2006, $584/month; in 2004, $578/month; and in 2000, $647/month based on Watson Wyatt calculations. Incidentally, remember that after both spouses die, the annuity terminates and the remaining invested assets revert to the institution that initially agreed to pay the monthly annuity payments.

CAUTION Annuities make sense in certain situations, but one needs to proceed with caution and avoid the hype that will probably come your way from insurance brokers and others as you grow older and draw closer to your retirement years. Clearly, do your research and compare, shop, and above all, don't invest unless you are clearly certain of what is contained in the contracts you are signing.

You should live so long

Longevity Insurance is a new concept that only a small number of insurance companies are offering. Like an annuity, this insurance allows for monthly payouts based on a lump-sum contribution that you make when you are 55 or older. The payouts begin at the age of 80 or more and are based on the amount of the lump-sum contribution, the age you make the

contribution, the age you choose for the payouts to start, inflation rates, death benefits to heirs and other options. Of course, the younger you are when the contribution is made, the larger the payouts will be. The payouts will continue as long as you live.
With insurers predicting that about 33% of boomers will make it into their 90's, the probability of running out of money is a large consideration.

This insurance will also allow you to withdraw a larger percentage of your savings at a younger age, knowing that you are covered by this type of safety net in your later years.

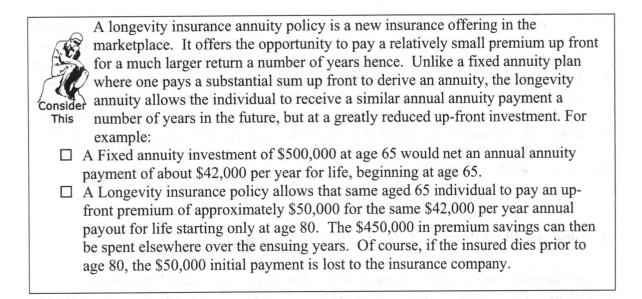

A longevity insurance annuity policy is a new insurance offering in the marketplace. It offers the opportunity to pay a relatively small premium up front for a much larger return a number of years hence. Unlike a fixed annuity plan where one pays a substantial sum up front to derive an annuity, the longevity annuity allows the individual to receive a similar annual annuity payment a number of years in the future, but at a greatly reduced up-front investment. For example:

Consider This

☐ A Fixed annuity investment of $500,000 at age 65 would net an annual annuity payment of about $42,000 per year for life, beginning at age 65.

☐ A Longevity insurance policy allows that same aged 65 individual to pay an up-front premium of approximately $50,000 for the same $42,000 per year annual payout for life starting only at age 80. The $450,000 in premium savings can then be spent elsewhere over the ensuing years. Of course, if the insured dies prior to age 80, the $50,000 initial payment is lost to the insurance company.

Do talk to your insurance consultant regarding this new product to determine if it is right for you. Just make sure if you decide to go this route that you will live long enough to enjoy it. That means paying close attention to the advice in the "Keeping in Shape" chapter.

Reverse mortgages are another source that can provide a retirement income stream

Reverse mortgages are loans that allow homeowners aged 62 and older to convert home equity into cash while living at home for as long as they want. Borrowers continue to own their homes, and do not make any monthly payments. Instead, they choose to receive funds as a lump sum, line of credit, or monthly payments (for up to the rest of their lives). The loan becomes due only when the borrower moves out, dies, or sells the home. In other words, the borrower continues living in their home, and is actually paid money against the value of the property.

?

Did You Know? Reverse Mortgages can relieve financial pressures, but The National Council on Aging found that although 2/3 of those over 62 have heard of the reverse mortgages, only 9% indicate they are likely to use this financing method to pay for home health care and other financial needs. Many worry about the risk of impoverishment without a home, or the loss of the legacy of a home that their children could use if they tap home equity. Also, the cost of these loans, and current Medicaid policies on how reverse mortgages affect eligibility for long-term care benefits appear as barriers.

The amount one can receive is dependent on several factors including one's age, the value of the home (often one cannot borrow against the entire value of the property), current interest rates, and the specific plan chosen. As a rule of thumb, the older the person is and the higher the property value, the more that can be borrowed. The borrower always retains title to the property. A reverse mortgage is actually a lien just like a conventional mortgage.

To learn more, one can call the National Reverse Mortgage Lenders Association at 1-866-264-4466 (toll-free) for a copy of their booklet, "Just the FAQ's: Answers to Common Questions about Reverse Mortgages".

Happiness will be there, but you need to make it happen

It is not surprising to learn that those with higher financial security rank higher with life satisfaction. They are more socially involved and see themselves generally as happier than those struggling with finances. For them, and hopefully for you, it is a question of balance to feed your needs, whether these relate to body, mind or spirit.

As stated earlier, if you plan for your financial security, and use your skills, knowledge and ability to become financially savvy, you will become financially comfortable in your retirement, which will go a long way to greater fulfillment and happiness. You will be more able to transcend difficulties, find personal growth, achieve a more complete life balance and pursue plans tied to your own unique desires.

CHAPTER 2

PATH 2: THE FINANCIAL PICTURE…MAKING IT A MASTERPIECE

EXERCISES

If you have not already done so, now is your opportunity to complete the following exercises which will prove helpful to understanding your knowledge in this financial security and planning arena, as well helping you to consider dealing with alternative situations and opportunities.

Exercise 1: Self-Testing: Your Knowledge About Financial Matters

Exercise 2: Determining How You Feel and Think About Your Financial Planning For Retirement

Exercise 3: Financial "PEACE" Exercise…"PEACE = **P**onder **E**verything **A**nd **C**heck **E**ssentials (for a Better Planned Tomorrow)

Exercise 4: Beyond Necessities: How You Plan To Spend Your Savings

ADDENDUM:

For Those Believing They Have Insufficient Money to Live Sufficiently In Retirement

At the conclusion of the exercises **and Addendum** is a "**Summary of Decisions**" page, which will allow you to think through some of the thoughts and ideas you have been gathering in completing this chapter. Please take some time to evaluate the information you have both reviewed and created and then summarize some key points, in writing, that you would like to pursue in putting together your final action plan in this book's last chapter, **"Your Action Plan…Putting It All Together"**.

EXERCISE 1

SELF-TESTING: YOUR KNOWLEDGE ABOUT FINANCIAL MATTERS

Fill in the blanks: (Answers on next page)

1. The economy's _____ rate will have a major impact upon your portfolio's value over the coming years.

2. Asset _____ is a key determinant of how to divide your portfolio.

3. One way to protect against a major medical or health drain on savings in retirement is to have a _____ term care policy.

4. Some people purchase an _____ from an insurance company that pays out a pre-established amount to them in retirement, typically on a monthly basis.

5. A _____ Financial Counselor or an _____ can assist you with financial planning in anticipation of your retirement.

6. Having "critical mass" refers to having _____ funds to replenish your portfolio for your needs without having to work in retirement.

7. Avoiding _____ is often more important in retirement then generating returns on your savings.

8. In determining expected returns and actions to be taken, experts use _____ tables to determine a person's annuity payouts.

9. A person's spending _____ and the quality of their health are two of the largest determinants of their financial well being in retirement.

10. According to the Bureau of Labor, 79% of Boomers see themselves _____ in retirement.

11. Experts indicate that if after retirement, you restrict your withholdings to ___ % of your portfolio in the first year of retirement and increase this amount by the rate of _____ , your savings should last your entire lifetime.

12. As a rule of thumb, financial experts indicate that you can live adequately in retirement, with lifetime savings, defined pensions, social security, and earnings generating receipts equaling ____-____% of your pre-retirement net income.

Answers to the 12 questions:

1. inflation
2. allocation
3. long
4. annuity
5. 2 answers: Certified & accountant
6. sufficient
7. risk
8. life expectancy
9. habits
10. working
11. 2 answers: 4% & inflation
12. 70 – 80%

Feedback relating to the exercise:

12 of 12 = You are financially savvy about your retirement finances.

9 + of 12= You are reasonably knowledgeable and probably have qualified to work on your own or with a professional advisor in preparing for retirement.

7+ of 12= You probably understand the basics of your financial situation in anticipation of retirement, but you need to either study more or get an expert to assist you in planning financially for your retirement.

4+ of 12= You need to study/learn the basics and seek out a financial consultant and coach as soon as possible.

0 to 3= Seriously begin to read more, listen to shows that discuss investing, and seek an advisor of others you trust who can suggest a really good accountant or advisor to help with your finances.

[Please return to page 35 to continue reading Chapter 2.]

EXERCISE 2:

DETERMINING HOW YOU FEEL AND THINK ABOUT YOUR FINANCIAL PLANNING FOR RETIREMENT

Please complete the following exercise by marking each as either True or False:

When I think about retirement:

1. My spouse/partner and I are on the same page about our retirement plans.

2. When planning the financial aspects of my retirement, I am comfortable using a financial counselor.

3. I will have more freedom to do activities like financially planning my portfolio or doing leisure activities in retirement.

4. My children will not be a burden in retirement.

5. I have anticipated and planned the need to modify my housing needs over time in retirement.

6. I have a positive attitude about my retirement years.

7. I will be able to travel well in retirement because I planned ahead.

8. I anticipate buying what I desire in retirement.

9. I anticipate buying what I need in retirement.

10. I have made plans to cover my health needs in years to come.

11. I have made plans to live in the right location to be accessible to friends and family.

12. I have taken account of inflation in my retirement estimates.

13. I have anticipated having sufficient funds to last for my retirement years or, better still, I plan to leave a financial legacy following my passing.

14. I know where I can get sound financial accounting and financial support, when needed.

15. I know where I can get sound legal assistance, when needed.

16. Aging is more a matter of attitude than time.

17. I am becoming smarter and wiser, not just older, as I age.

(It would also be wise to have your spouse/partner complete this exercise, to determine if you are on "the same page.")

How to score this exercise:

This exercise is designed to provide realistic feedback to you. Although you completed the exercise, you also identified your state of preparation and state of mind relating to your projected financial status in retirement. How can this be?

First, according to researchers, the more one looks forward to retirement and has a positive attitude toward aging, the greater a person's chances of living longer. Second, the more one plans ahead for their well-being in retirement, the greater the chance for having the financial wherewithal to attain a happy retirement. Therefore, two points should be drawn from the exercise above:

1. The more statements marked as true, the more likely that you will meet your retirement needs when they arrive.

2. Those statements indicated as not true should be further investigated. Numbers 6, 16 and 17 speak to your attitude and should be positive for the reasons mentioned above. The remaining statements marked false should be further examined as they point to areas that need action; these answers marked false reflect issues that need further review toward making your retirement as fulfilling as you would hope it to be.

[Please return to page 37 to continue reading Chapter 2.]

EXERCISE 3

FINANCIAL "PEACE"…PEACE = PONDER EVERYTHING AND CHECK ESSENTIALS (for a Better Planned Tomorrow)

Below, you will see a Bingo-like card, much as you would see in any bingo game. In this game, the objective is to obtain "PEACE" of mind and eventually put an X or a completion checkmark through every corresponding letter—number item such as P1, P2, P3 and so forth, with the intention of completing the entire card. An "X" through each letter/number combination symbolizes that you have completed the actions associated with that item. Put a "0" next to the number to signify that you want/need to work on this item. Put a "NA" next to the number to identify those items that do not apply to your situation. No one will likely see your progress so be honest with yourself and score your actions accordingly. Only you will know if you are preparing yourself for your future and that of your loved ones.

P	E	A	C	E
P1	E7	A13	C19	E25
P2	E8	A14	C20	E26
P3	E9	A15	C21	E27
P4	E10	A16	C22	E28
P5	E11	A17	C23	E29
P6	E12	A18	C24	E30

P1 I sat down with my attorney and sought their legal advice in preparation for retirement. A will was drawn up and signed.
P2 With my attorney, a living will and Medical Power of Attorney was drawn up and signed.
P3 With my attorney, a Power of Attorney was drawn up and signed.
P4 I considered creating an executive trust for my estate and depending on the size of my estate and my attorney's advice, I followed through on this as was deemed appropriate.
P5 I chose an executor for my will and they agreed to perform these duties. I also sent them the location of my will and if appropriate, my trust documents.
P6 I recorded all my worldly possessions on a video or CD storing it in a safe place (safe deposit box or with a person I can trust) and determined to whom I would leave each item upon my death.

E7 I developed a record on all my financial matters so that it can be easily found and used to address my needs upon incapacitation or upon my death.
E8 I documented and stored my bond certificates.
E9 I documented in one place the location of my bank accounts.
E10 I documented in one place the location of my credit card numbers.
E11 I documented in one place the location of life insurance policy numbers.
E12 I documented in one place the location of pre-funeral payments and burial site ownership.

A13 I documented in one place the location of a list of the institutions that hold my financial portfolios.

A14 I documented in one place the location of the names of my financial consultants who help me manage my money.

A15 I documented in one place the location of my real estate holdings.

A16 I documented in one place the location of my mortgage payments or my mortgage completion records.

A17 I documented in one place the location of my tax records, prior year income tax and 1040 records.

A18 I documented in one place the location of my vehicle ownership records.

C19 I documented in one place the location of my homeowners and vehicle insurance records.

C20 I examined whether a Long-Term Care Insurance plan is something that makes sense for me (See below for comments on this.) *

C21 I reviewed my current medical and hospital insurance coverage, real estate insurance and other insurance to ensure it is sufficient to cover me and my dependents when needed, protecting me against significant future loss.

C22 I reviewed my life insurance coverage to insure that I have sufficient coverage to meet future needs.

C23 I reviewed my need for salary continuance insurance by judging the probability of occurrence, i.e. performing a risk assessment. **

C24 I developed a back-up plan to secure insurance in the event of separation from my employer.

E25 I have also established a separate insurance policy to cover a payment to my executor for the performance of these duties in the event of my death. I have had my executor sign bank entry signature cards so they can quickly gain access to bank vault deposits and secured documents in case of emergency or death.

E26 I know how to contact my previous employers and the military (if applicable) to ascertain and receive the amounts of defined pension plan or veteran benefits that would be owed to me. I have good knowledge of the amounts and choices of options provided by my former employer or the military. ***

E27 I have contacted the Social Security Administration to understand my government entitlements projected to the day I plan to receive them.

E28 I have looked into reverse mortgages, understand how they operate and know where to get them should this ever prove necessary.

E29 If I have sufficient funds, I have put money aside for my grandchildren's education and planned my estate so that money will be set aside for my children, grandchildren, and charity. I have also examined the value of donating monies to these individuals while I live (with the resultant recognition of my generosity). Conversely, if I have insufficient monies for these purposes, I have made this fact known to those who might otherwise expect such monies.

E30 I have written my own obituary to reflect in my own words what I would like to have communicated. I have also made my funeral arrangements. Finally, I have written personal legacy documents to those with whom I would like to communicate my thoughts, sometimes referred to as an "Ethical Will."

* Purchasing Long-Term Care Insurance, like the purchase of all insurance, is a matter of estimating risk, i.e. in this case a chance that there will be a need for home health care or nursing care, which can largely eradicate life-long savings, versus saving the premium costs and chancing the probability that such care will not be needed. Contacting insurance providers, such as Northwestern Mutual, John Hancock or other providers, will give the prospective retiree specific costs and coverage details. As a benchmark, the insurance industry states that one in three individuals will require long term care during their lifetime, although the typical duration is for less than 90 days. Costs for services range typically from $150-$250 a day although such costs continue to rise with inflation. Nursing care residency can last for years, but most often a stay will be under five years. Longer stays add up to big dollar expenditures. The younger one is when purchasing the coverage, the smaller the annual premiums. Also note that if one suffers certain medical conditions, long-term care insurance coverage will not be offered to those individuals, another good reason to consider purchasing it in one's younger years.

** In judging risk of salary continuance, note that often such insurance is provided by one's employer. Upon separation from an employer or upon retirement, such insurance will likely not be available to the employee.

*** If a pension is due, one should learn what choices one would have in how one could receive it…as a lump sum payment, as a year certain, or as a joint survivorship upon a spouse's death. Unfortunately, many planning retirement wait until just a few months before retirement to learn of their entitlement, not realizing that this is vital information to know in determining one's cash flow in retirement. Be sure to keep in touch with your former employers and remember that companies merge or are acquired with possible resultant changes to staff compositions, benefit administrators and so forth.

[Please return to page 45 to continue reading Chapter 2.]

EXERCISE 4

BEYOND NECESSITIES: HOW YOU PLAN TO SPEND YOUR SAVINGS

Individuals have their own perceptions of what is a necessity and on what they will spend their money. Necessities typically include food, clothing, transportation, a place to live, utilities (heat, electricity, telephone), medications, and good old taxes. Other ongoing items that many consider essentials include cable/dish network, and broadband (internet conductivity).

Here is a starting list for other non-recurring expenditures that one may identify as priority items:
- Contributing to church/synagogue
- Contributing to non-profit charities
- Contributions for grandchildren's college education
- Money given to assist children in maintaining their standards of living
- Money for elderly parents
- For travel or vacations
- Purchasing a second home, a rental, an RV, or a time share
- For cosmetic or elective surgery
- Rehabbing current residence
- Purchasing antiques or other collectibles
- Purchasing electronics or other "fun" items
- Purchasing a new more expensive automobile

On What Do I Plan To Spend My Disposable Income?   How many $s?

1st Priority

2nd Priority

3rd Priority

4th Priority

5th Priority

6th Priority

7th Priority

8th Priority

[Please return to page 46 to continue reading Chapter 2.]

ADDENDUM

FOR THOSE BELIEVING THEY HAVE INSUFFICIENT MONEY TO LIVE SUFFICIENTLY IN RETIREMENT

"It is the heart that makes a man rich. He is rich according to what he is, not according to what he has."
Henry Ward Beecher (1813-1887) American politician

Earlier in this chapter, we commented on the fact that a lot of money to one person could represent little money to another person. It depends on the lifestyle they have become accustomed to or wish to have following retirement. To illustrate the point further, as it relates to working in retirement, let us review the following scenarios. First, we have one couple who had saved $75,000 for retirement and thought their life was wonderful. They do not think they need to work for money. By living the simple life, they get to read books, live in a nice small apartment that is easy to keep clean and is close to places to do their grocery shopping. They get to watch lots of TV, go for long walks and to an occasional movie, eat at a fast food restaurant or visit the library, visit with friends locally, play cards, volunteer at a local church, baby sit for their grandchild and "enjoy life". Both individuals are clearly happy to be retired with the lifestyle they believe is free from want and worry to do what they desire.

Conversely, another individual feels he will never have sufficient money in retirement, even though he has amassed over seven million dollars in retirement savings. He thinks he wants to be able to spend several hundred thousand a year to enjoy his planned lifestyle of top of the line travel, boating, seeing the latest names in theater performances and he is disappointed he needs to work to get enough "to live on."

In the two examples above, it is a matter of attitude that determines whether one will need to work.

On the other hand, there are those who clearly have insufficient funds to support themselves in their retirement years. If they do not work or get money or assistance, they will be unable to pay for their food, shelter, medicines, health plan premiums, taxes, utilities, health care, medicines, transportation, and so forth. Their cash flow is needed to subsist. It seems that without working, they will fall into or increase their indebtedness.

You are not alone

"Many of the things you can count, don't count. Many of the things you can't count, really count."
Albert Einstein (1879-1955) German-Swiss-U.S. scientist

If you are questioning whether you will be able to afford living in retirement, rest assured, you are not alone. According to the Principal Financial Well-Being Index™ Survey:

- 42% of workers fear they will not enjoy the same quality of life they now have when in retirement.
- Some 43% of employees in small and midsize businesses, and 26% of retirees, are so anxious about being able to afford their future medical expenses in retirement that that they lose sleep over it.
- 38% fear they will not be able to afford the basic necessities of retirement, a concern that is particularly common among women.
- 37% of those already retired fear that inflation will erode their purchasing power over time.
- Yet…only 51% of retirees and 30% of current employees have a plan for turning their investments into bills paid.

And to make matters worse, the following additional statistics show the magnitude of the problem:

1. Only about a fifth of full time employees have a traditional pension plan and those numbers are declining daily.
2. Less than one in ten of all employees contribute to an IRA on their own outside of work.
3. Approximately half of all private-sector employees don't have access to a 401(K) or other company-sponsored investment plans or have decided not to make contributions to such a plan because they generally are strapped for funds in meeting their daily living expenses.
4. Of those contributing to a retirement plan, their average saving is less than $30,000, an amount insufficient to see them through their predicted ever-lengthening retirement years.

YEAR	Percentage of United States households saving and investing for retirement
2000	78%
2001	69%
2002	72%
2003	71%
2004	68%
2005	69%
2006	70%
2007	66%

Source: Employee Benefit Research Institute, 2007, Retirement Confidence Survey

According to this same Employee Benefit Research Institute 2007 Retirement Confidence Survey, those aged over 55 have NOT saved sufficiently to take care of their needs. Here are the figures:

Saved less than $10,000	26%
Saved $10,000 to $24, 999	5%
Saved $25,000 to $49,999	9%
Saved $50,000 to $99,999	11%
Saved $100,000 to $249,000	20%
Saved $250,000 or more	28%

Retirement Weekly, Barron's Magazine, (May 16, 2006) indicated 3 top reasons preventing 48% of working Americans from saving for retirement: 50% "barely had any money left after paying basic living expenses"; 27% said "any extra money was being used to pay off credit card debt;" and 26% "simply procrastinated."

The growing problem of debt

Credit cards issuers may be viewed as a major source of evil. Banks and their partners are constantly tempting us with free miles, free stays, free trips, bonus gifts, and so forth if we sign on and use their credit cards. The average American has numerous cards and many lines of credit. They also hold thousands of dollars of debt and are paying out unbelievably large, costly dollars to creditors, money that should be going to purchase food, housing, and other necessities. A recent study shows that among households with members 65 and older the average credit card debt is $4,907. Another AARP article (July and August 2007 "Avoiding Money Traps") stated that debt has risen from 56% of families headed by someone 55 or older in 2001 to 61% in 2004.

An article by Jordan Goodman in the May-June, 2007 <u>AARP Newsletter</u> titled, "Debt Relief: Beware the Frauds," subtitled "Can you cut your debt in an instant? Don't believe it. But real counseling will show you a way out," suggests that it is essential for individuals having debt issues to see a professional counselor to turn their situation around. They point out that a quick debt settlement is not the way to reduce debt and that working with a good counselor can help repair a person's credit rating. For a list of non-profit credit counseling services in your area, go to: The National Foundation for Credit Counseling 800-388-2227; <u>www.nfcc.org</u> and Association of Independent Consumer Credit Counseling Agencies 800-450-1794; <u>www.alcca.org</u>.

AARP suggests that if you have debt problems: 1. Find a reputable counselor and sit down with him/her to review your entire financial situation in detail…a 45 to 90 minute face-to-face conversation. 2. Develop a comprehensive plan together for removing the debt in an organized step-by-step fashion, with no quick fixes along the way.

TIPS

A happy retirement may be a distant dream for the estimated 28 million people nationally who do not have a checking or a savings account. It might also elude another 4.5 million who use banks only occasionally. These individuals often use check-cashing outlets which number about 6,500 across the country. To get money exchanged from other sources at check-cashing outlets typically costs an individual a substantial fee, ranging anywhere from 2%-12% per transaction (over a billion dollar boon for the check-cashing outlets). Why does all this take place instead of using a bank with little or no fee? The answer is that these vast numbers of individuals have had to contend with bounced checks and other transgressions and have been socked with expensive penalty fees. In view of increasing credit debt, other indebtedness, and increasing home foreclosures, the number of individuals burdened by financial issues will only increase (as will the check-cashing industry which has doubled since the mid-1990s.)

Dependence on Social Security

Today's retiree finds his/her primary source of income coming from Social Security followed by personal savings and a traditional employer-provided pension plan. Many retirees don't even fully comprehend how dependent they are on Social Security in the daily management of their retirement budgets.

In the future, the scenario of having Social Security payments be the primary source of retirement income will evolve and most Boomers appear to understand that. These facts are not to say that Social Security will disappear. Far from it, but changes to plan coverage and entitlement criteria could well change. Age qualifications could ratchet up as they have in the past. Means testing could also be put in place as could reduction criteria tied to income derived from other sources.

 Whereas many workers today expect to rely on savings in retirement as they probably well should. But, as shown in the table below, today's retirees receive 61% of their retirement funding from two sources: Social Security and employer-provided pensions. The issue for Boomers and the generations that follow is that knowledge of a need to save is not followed by what is actually being done.

Method of Financing One's Retirement	Retirees (reported)	Workers (expected)
Social Security	40%	14%
A traditional employer-provided pension	21%	13%
Personal Savings	24%	50%
Other personal savings or investments	18%	22%
A workplace retirement plan, such as a 401(K)	6%	28%
Employment	2%	11%
The sale or refinancing of your home	2%	2%
Something else	4%	3%
Don't know	5%	5%

Source: Employee Benefit Research Institute, Mathew Greenwald and Associates

Note that those who draw upon their Social Security at age 62 will suffer an estimated 25% reduction in benefits compared to waiting until one has reached the full retirement age. The break-even point is about age 81, at which point the amount received will add up to the same amount regardless of whether you opt for immediate or delayed income. In the years following age 81 the person who has waited will continue to receive a larger annual payout. Also note, if you receive early Social Security payments, the government reduces your payout by a dollar for every 2 dollars you earn from working. You are permitted to earn up to $13,560 (the 2008 number) without penalty. When you reach the full retirement age, the penalty for earning income is removed. Financial consultants suggest that you defer your social security payments as long as possible up to age 70, at which point you receive your maximum entitlements.

The US ranks in the bottom third of a group of 30 industrial countries in terms of the size of its Social Security payments. Other countries provide much higher Social Security-like payouts as a percent of worker pre-retirement earnings. In some cases payouts almost match previous full-time worker income, and in the case of one European country (Luxembourg) they exceed previous earnings. How is this possible? The answer: taxes. In the USA, funding for Social Security comes only from workers and employers, not from additional taxes.

Work can be a gift

"Happiness is not a goal, it is a by-product."
Eleanor Roosevelt (1884-1962) First Lady of the United States, columnist, lecturer and humanitarian

As pointed out in many recent surveys, most Boomers are not looking to emulate their parents' type of retirement, i.e. living the "leisure lifestyle" paradigm. In some cases it is because they fear they will have insufficient funds, but in many other cases they desire to work in retirement. Three of four Boomers, perhaps more, plan to work in some capacity in retirement. Interestingly, many recent retirees over the past decade have also transitioned into retirement by working on a full or part-time basis. In some cases, this continued work was chosen, not out of a sense of needing additional funds, but rather to fill a void...to fulfill a passion, to continue being active, to continue relationships or to meet other people, to continue being creative, or to simply "stay out of the hair " of their spouse or partner. Additionally, working people today understand that work also has its own rewards in keeping us sharp, more current and worldly, and it provides opportunity for achievement. Finally, for those having difficulty transitioning from their "working world" identity and structure, working in retirement provides such individuals with a purpose and a structure for managing their lives.

Many individuals wait too long before dealing with the issue of what type of work they will perform in retirement. They struggle with what occupation they will want to have, avoiding investigating options, often until they are virtually into retirement or are forced through termination by employers to make choices (finding themselves in "early retirement.")

Should an individual work in the same field as before, perhaps for less money or part-time, or should they pursue a "second career". Some struggle alone with this dilemma. Others seek out assistance from career counselors or coaches. It comes down to choices...choices...choices.

And now comes some advice: It is best to examine options early and see what is out there that can fill your desires or needs. This means begin taking action, perhaps as early as 7 - 10 years before retirement. Do your research. Speak to others in your new field of interest. Learn, study (perhaps taking classes) or work in your new chosen field on a part-time basis. Experiment. Look at this period as a time of exploration, and invest the time. Look at it as a time, much like you did earlier, when you were in your late teens and 20's, determining your future occupation. If you want to open a bed and breakfast, or become an entrepreneur, or learn how to become a good golfer, start early. Don't be reactive to what others bring your way...Control your future work destiny yourself.

More importantly, until age 65, many people who would really like to retire are forced to continue working in order to secure health insurance. Often, although a continuation of income is desirable, many consider it even more important to have medical coverage until Medicare is available (at age 65). Obviously, especially if one is ill or becomes ill, the fear is to be among the 48 million without medical coverage. A critical date is arriving at age 63 1/2 while one is employed. Were one to lose a job at that juncture, a person would typically qualify for COBRA coverage for up to 18 months upon being terminated; this is not to suggest that this is a good situation because although coverage continuance would be there, COBRA coverage is very expensive. Finally, a word about medical coverage after reaching age 65: experts advise enrolling in one of a number of available supplemental insurance plans to help pay the costs that Medicare does not cover.

As stated earlier in this chapter and in other chapters, employees have personally experienced a reduction in retirement benefits. In fact, the Employee Benefit Research Institute (EBRI) has found in their surveys that in the past 2 years, one-sixth of all employees have found this to be true. Remarkably, as far back as August 1986, in an article from the *Personnel Administrator*, titled "Retirement; Crisis or Opportunity," the authors, Eugene H. Seibert and Joanne Seibert, pointed out that reducing costs was already a trend. "Being lean and cost-effective will continue to be major priorities for many companies…rarely have so many axes sliced into business at a time of economic growth." As part of this trend, companies were encouraging older (more expensive) workers to retire early, as evidenced in the same article: "Efforts to discourage older workers from retiring before age 65 or to encourage them to postpone retirement beyond age 65 are exceedingly rare."

If you believe you will work in retirement, it isn't surprising, because as stated in other places in this book, the vast majority of Boomers plan to work in retirement, unlike previous generations of retirees. If you want to work, but need not work, than that is fine…perhaps wonderful…as it is your choice. Hopefully, enjoy it, grow and learn from it, and of course, we hope you accomplish what you desire.

Besides money, what do older workers seek in the company they work for? Surprisingly, older workers prize a variety of benefits according to the Three River Workforce Investment Board. These include: Employee assistance and work-life programs, elder-care assistance, retirement and financial planning, integrating adaptive and assistive technology in the workplace, integrating ergonomic adjustments in the workplace, health-care for less than full-time employment, and opportunities to mentor younger workers.

Other Sources of Income

You Decide Are there alternatives to working if one does not have sufficient money to live through a week, month, or longer periods? Is work the only means to stay ahead of "the collector" and make "ends meet"? What happens if one is unable to work or to find a sufficient paying job to meet the cash flow requirements believed to be there? In situations such as these, visit with agencies and volunteer organizations that can assist those in need.

The following are some initial methods for finding sources of money as alternatives to working. Obviously, taking on greater debt is the biggest hurdle to becoming self-sufficient in retirement or in life.

- If you own a property or possessions you can live without, consider selling them.
- If you own a house that you are not fully using, consider moving into a smaller place or renting a home or apartment.
- If you own a home and paid off the mortgage, consider applying for a reverse mortgage and use these funds to meet your needs. You may avoid needing to move.
- Consider moving to a location that has lower taxes.
- Some have rented out a room or taken in a roommate (be careful with your choices here as this choice could be regretted.)
- Consider moving to a more rural location where cost of living is lower or move to a location where temperatures are more moderate with corresponding lower utility rates.
- Consider sharing an automobile or not having one and using mass transportation, or traveling less.
- Veterans should contact the Veterans Administration to learn about assistance such as medical discounts, hospital services, etc.
- Examine what local voluntary and governmental agencies can provide. For example, consider signing up for food stamps, visiting the local food pantry, or applying for meals through "Meals on Wheels."
- Speak confidentially to your priest, rabbi, or other member of the clergy, who could possibly assist you. Perhaps helping your church could result in some assistance by exchanging your time and talent for necessities.
- Take advantage of all senior discount programs; for example always ask about discounts on haircuts, reductions on property taxes and public transit charges, entrance fees, etc.
- Comparative shop, spend less, and/or substitute cheaper for more expensive, for example, by buying less expensive cuts of meats or going meatless. Buy items on sale and store them for when they are needed; for example, buying meat in bulk and freezing cuts for later use.
- Buy at discounters like Wal-Mart, Costco, or TJ Maxx or Marshals. Consider buying at garage sales, at second hand clothing stores, or avoid buying new clothes altogether.
- Trim vacation plans, eat meals out less often or not at all, and find alternatives to paid recreation (that charge fees or dues.)
- Cancel services like Cable TV, Premium Channels, and places like health clubs.
- Apply for special medical prescription cards through the drug manufacturers themselves. Choose generic drugs where possible. Often ordering in bulk and via the Internet can provide big savings, but be careful and check for quality.
- If needed, examine alternative nursing care programs. Costs vary widely for similar services (public assistance [such as Medicaid] is available, providing the individual can qualify, and these services may closely approximate private more expensive care.)

- Examine your insurance policies to ensure you are not over-insured. Expensive life insurance, disability insurance, mortgage insurance, or certain levels of mortgage insurance that may have been needed to ensure safety while children were being raised, may not be needed later in retirement.

The list is only an illustration of what can be done to finance one's way toward a less intensive "work required existence" in retirement. Speak to friends, colleagues, agencies, and even "fee based" advisors to learn about other alternatives to working in retirement.

Conversely, as indicated above, there are alternatives to working full time or for the rest of your life. Even supposing that you don't collect a pension, find social security payments wanting, and lack sufficient savings to meet your needs upon entering retirement, you may be able to find help from other sources. America is a country full of generous people who have the means of serving the greater good and the greater need of others. If you fall into the position of needing help or need to make choices to sustain your lifestyle, do not hesitate to investigate alternatives to holding a job.

"That every day has its pains and sorrows is universally experienced, and almost universally confessed: but let us not attend only to mournful truths; if we look impartially about us, we shall find that every day has likewise its pleasures and its joys"
Samuel Johnson (1709-1759) writer

Retirement means "freedom"; it is a time when one can really make choices. It is also a time for fulfilling "dreams" and gaps in one's life. Look at retirement as an opportunity to use your time wisely to fulfill your needs because it is you that has this ONE LIFETIME. Make it a lifetime you can feel pride in. If you must work, then use it toward feeling fulfilled, or if you cannot find fulfillment in your work, then use your free remaining time to find happiness in what else you do. Work can be a means as well as an end goal.

Be Optimistic: some facts may surprise you

"Money will buy a bed but not sleep; books but not brains; food but not appetite; finery but not beauty; a house but not a home; medicine but not health; luxuries but not culture; amusements but not happiness; religion but not salvation; a passport to everywhere but heaven."
Anonymous

Do your thoughts make you happy? Optimists tend to have a set of traits that make them happy. Cultivating a mindset that features the positive aspects of one's life and being thankful for them tends to make its way into it becoming a self-fulfilling prophesy.

Is it that happy people are optimists or that optimists tend to be happy people? They tend to have a habitual internal control mechanism that focuses on their ability to be master of their own fate, (not feeling victims of circumstance). This internal control mechanism is not simply an attempt to look at the world "through rose-colored glasses" although they can be filled with too much optimism. Their internal control mechanism is driven by a pragmatic ability to "problem-solve" and find solutions to stressors and challenges. Optimists tend to come up with practical solutions and feel uplifted (buoyant) by the progress they make. They are more realistic and rational than pessimists. They tend to see negative events or situations as a temporary setback, and to see a setback as affecting only a small arena of their lives or self-worth.

As described in March 2007 *AARP Magazine*, in an article titled, "Pessimists Who Think Life Can Only Get Worse Can Only Be Right." Denis Boyles points out that Optimists are generally careful and do not blame themselves for issues that may have a variety of causes. In being happy, they become "cheerleaders" when this approach may not always be appropriate. Optimists typically work very hard, have many ideas, and tend to be creative. Work, wild ideas, and optimism drive progress; so too for a long life. That was proven in a recent study finding that optimists live longer than pessimists, have fewer heart attacks, and experience less pain.

Dr. Norman Vincent Peale, in his book published over 50 years ago titled, *"The Power of Positive Thinking"*, mixed natural psychological thoughts with religiously-based principles to help individuals address the various concerns they had for managing the aspects of daily life. He encouraged readers to develop a mental picture of success for themselves. He said, "If God be for us, who can be against us?" He cautioned individuals not to build obstacles in their imaginations and instead to examine difficulties for what they are…resolvable, to be dealt with on a focused basis.

Subject	Information on Optimists
Brain Research	Recent research has proven that optimism activates two brain areas known as the amygdala and the rostral anterior cingulated cortex, both of which sit in the middle of the brain; when positive events occur, these areas become activated.
On Aging	Among aging populations, those with a more positive attitude were not only healthier but more active
On how they carry themselves	They truly tend to walk faster and hold their bodies more erect.
In Business	No successful individual could manage business by thinking they will lose money and go bankrupt.

Again, Denis Boyles in his *AARP Magazine* article also presented the following interesting material: Optimism varies with age, and to illustrate the point, the magazine provided the following fun item:

- At age 50: "The world's going to the dogs!"
- At age 75: "It's amazing the things they can do".
- At age 100: "Ah! Another day without a major asteroid strike!"

And also this amusing chart:

Activity	Level of Optimism (out of ten)
Dating	
Age 20-29	8.25
Age 30-39	7.75
Age 40-64	2.0
Age 65-100	9.85
Golf	
Hole 1	9.95
Hole 18	0.5
Finance	
Wall Street	5.0
Las Vegas	10.0
Diet	
1st 5 pounds	9.0
Last pound	-3.6

And finally, the title of the *AARP Magazine* article itself says: "Pessimists who think life can only get worse can only be right". Mr. Boyles points out how "pessimism, like black holes in space, swallow everything surrounding them...it resembles a magnet that swallows one day after another until there are no days left".

So, you choose. You decide. Have faith, you can find happiness if you believe you can do so. Join the optimists and take action, and take comfort in knowing, "Optimists are not always happy, but they always think they might be soon."

SUMMARY OF DECISIONS

PATH 2: MAKING YOUR FINANCIAL PICTURE A MASTERPIECE

Now that you have some background on the topic of "**Making Your Financial Picture a Masterpiece**" and have completed the exercises in this chapter, you should have reached some personal decisions which will later become **key toward completing your final Action Plan in Chapter 8.** Think about what you would like **to do more of,** or perhaps, what you would like to **do less of** in preparing for your most realistic and fulfilling retirement. Consider in what capacity you see yourself changing your financial goals and actions in the future and why.

 You Decide What do I want to commit to working on related to my vision of a successful retirement?

1.   I would like continue exploring the financial information that I need in order to transition successfully into retirement.

2.   Based on the exercises that I completed, I would like to share some of the findings I discovered with a financial advisor, attorney, insurance broker, and other knowledgeable individuals and follow up to further assess where matters stand as well as seek their assistance where needed.

3.   I would like to build on the exercises that I completed, and follow through on specific steps I have already taken and also pursue those that yet need to be taken to have a financially successful retirement.

4.   If I believe I have insufficient funds saved for retirement, I would like to further identify alternatives beyond just continuing to work in retirement.

What are your **key decisions?**

Key Decision A

_____

_____

Key Decision B

_____

_____

Key Decision C

_____

_____

Other thoughts, questions, ideas, research that needs to be done, etc.:
Please transfer your decisions into Chapter 8 (Page 228): "Your Action Plan."

CHAPTER 3

PATH 3: KEEPING IN SHAPE

"The first wealth is health."
Ralph Waldo Emerson, "Power," *The Conduct of Life*

In this chapter, you will have the opportunity to:

1. Examine the importance of specific actions you can take to improve your chances for continued good health.
2. Learn or confirm information borne out by research that healthy aging is largely a product of what you do, i.e. it is much more than your genetics.
3. Through self-assessment exercises, you can determine how you can build a healthy physical and mental style of living that will be helpful for your remaining years in retirement.

Live longer, Live healthier

Based on current life expectancy, chances are good that you will have the opportunity to enjoy a much longer retirement than your parents or grandparents. And since your health and fitness are critical determinants of the quality of your extended retirement years, it has become more important than ever to age well – physically, mentally, and spiritually.

According to adult change expert Dr. Frederic Hudson in his book, *The Adult Years: Mastering the Art of Self-Renewal,* "Healthy aging includes a positive attitude toward life, good stress-coping skills, health-promoting behaviors, human skills to deal with everyday problems of living, and the good fortune to avoid infectious diseases and serious injuries.

"Getting old, on the other hand, means taking on the characteristics that our society expects old people to have: losing interest in life, accepting the notion that it's too late to change, believing that life doesn't matter anymore, failing to set goals and commitments, losing a sense of surprise, and giving in to passivity and boredom."

Life Expectancies

Current Age	Additional Years— Male	Additional Years— Female
40	35	41
45	31	36
50	26	31
55	22	27
60	18	23
65	15	19
70	12	15

(Source: www.annuityadvantage.com, Life Expectancy Table)

"A man's health can be judged by which he takes two at a time – pills or stairs."
Joan Welsh, poet quoted on www.thinkexist.com

?
Did You Know?
Not only can you look forward to living longer than previous generations as life expectancy continues getting longer, this population will likely continue to grow as a percentage of the population. Planners and policy makers can count on this rapid growth, even though the exact numbers are not known for certain. For example, according to the U.S. Census Bureau, in 2000, 35 million were 65 and older, and that population rises to 40.2 by 2010, 54.6 million in 2020, 71.5 million in 2030 and 86.7 million by 2050. In 2000, 4.2 million people were aged 85 and older (defined as the oldest old); their number is projected to increase to almost 10 million by 2030 and to 21 million by 2050, accounting for nearly 1 in 4 older people!

The issue of life expectancy is being debated by scientists and researchers. The question is whether medical advances can continue to increase the numbers beyond age 100 and what will future age limits become.

Your choices make a difference

Staying healthy into your 90s or beyond is no longer a pipe dream, given advances in medicine and a seemingly constant stream of research findings on steps you can take to build and maintain health.

Although good longevity genes never hurt, research shows that:
• 25% of your health is related to your genetic makeup
• 75% of how healthy you are is under your control

The belief that health inevitably declines as you age is common but misguided. In reality, people of any age can improve their health by adopting healthy behaviors. According to the Centers for Disease Control, maintaining just three healthy habits – moderate physical activity, good nutrition and no smoking – has a huge positive impact.

According to the National Institute on Aging (NIA), while the prevalence of risky health-related behavior is lower among older people, such behaviors do continue and do affect life-expectancy. Smoking, overuse of alcohol, lack of exercise, being overweight, not seeing a physician when symptoms arise, and inadequate consumption of fruits and vegetables are some of these risk behaviors.

Did You Know? The NIA also indicates that sixty-four percent of older adults between ages 65-74 are married and live with a spouse, but by age 85, 24 percent are married and live with a spouse, and 48 percent live alone. Married people have lower mortality rates than unmarried people at all ages, and it has been argued that the marriage advantage has a protective effect because married people are less likely to indulge in high-risk and health-damaging behavior, while also finding they are more likely to receive care and support when needed. Marriage may also open a network of extended relatives and friends.

With the increase in life expectancy and a simultaneous rise in the number of people with chronic diseases and disability, the issue for researchers is how to gain more disability-free years into individuals' later years. Among researchers the question of quality of life is referred to as "active life expectancy" (ALE), i.e. being active without disability. In 1990 (and with medical advances, the numbers have since improved) among those age 65, women could expect 9.8 years of disability–free years and men 7.4 years out of their remaining life expectancies. Disability among the older population is definitely declining, but women have a steeper rate of functional decline in old age, while men appear to have a higher likelihood of recovery following onset of a disability.

Taking care of yourself may be something you have found difficult for any number of reasons, ranging from insufficient time to lack of motivation. If that is true in your case, you might want to think of this next phase of life as a golden opportunity to focus on your physical, mental, and spiritual health. After all, as the saying goes, "the goal is to die feeling young and as late as possible."

 In **Exercise 1 (page 89),** "Where Are You Now, Where Are You Going," you are asked by a series of questions whether you are well focused on maintaining your physical, mental, and social health. Taking this simple quiz will give you a sense for areas where you might want to further spend your time and energy. If you completed it, how do you feel you did?

Health does *not* inevitably decline as you age.

"The only exercise some people get is jumping to conclusions, running down their friends, side-stepping responsibility, and pushing their luck!"
Anonymous

No more excuses – get moving

You
Decide
There's no getting around it – if you want to stay healthy, your routine needs to include at least 30 minutes of moderate physical activity most days of the week. You've probably heard it all before, but it's worth repeating. Being physically active can significantly reduce your risk of dying of heart disease, and decrease your risk of obesity, diabetes, high blood pressure, osteoporosis, stroke, and colon cancer. Plus, it can reduce the need for hospitalization, physician visits, and medications. And it positively affects your mental health as well as your physical well-being by combating anxiety and depression and dramatically reducing your risk of Alzheimer's.

A 2000 National Health Interview Survey (NHIS) provides information on general levels of activity during non-leisure time as well as usual daily activity related to moving around and to lifting and carrying things. Results show that physical activity decreases with age, with the 65 and older population about 5 times less likely to be physically active than those 18 to 24. According to a study by Barnes and Scheoenborn in 2003, older women are more likely than men to be inactive.

Four types of exercise are key:

- Aerobic activity (a.k.a. cardiorespiratory or cardiovascular) leads to more efficient energy production by cells and reduces the formation of potentially damaging free radicals. Among its many benefits, it helps prevent heart disease and stroke, and can help protect you against viral illnesses.
- Strength training is vital for building and maintaining the muscle mass everyone begins losing at age 30. It also helps improve balance, and is critical to avoiding injury and easily performing everyday tasks.
- Flexibility training – stretching – keeps your joints flexible so you can move freely, comfortably, and without pain.
- Exercise using weights is essential for overall muscle strength and retaining bone structure, a key to avoiding osteoporosis.

According to NHIS, walking is the most common (and one of the easiest) forms of activity among all age groups including older Americans.

Some people exercise with more intensity than others, no matter what their age. If you're involved in running, swimming, triathlons, or other sports where people continue to compete as they age, you know that the numbers of competitors over 60 and well into their 70s and 80s continue to grow. Gone are the days when you could count on earning an age-group medal simply for showing up and competing.

But you don't need to be a competitive athlete, or even exercise strenuously, to gain the benefits of physical activity. Whether it's walking with friends, biking, dancing, gardening, or skiing, find activities that you like – and do them regularly.

"Fitness - if it came in a bottle, everybody would have a great body."
Cher, actress and vocalist (1946--)

In Exercise 2 (page 91), "Excuses, Excuses, Excuses", you are asked to determine the extent that you fall into the trap that many, if not most individuals fall into, when determining if they have the inner drive and perseverance to take on the challenges that fall before them. In a matter of a minute or two, you can check off the quotes that apply to you and see where you stand. If you completed the exercise, what did you find? Confirmation or some new insights into what you might need to do differently? How would you begin and when?

According to several studies, the higher the education and income level, the greater the physical activity and also the greater one's happiness in retirement (even when disabilities are present.)

"Take care of your body. It's the only place you have to live."
Jim Rohn, author, coach, motivational speaker

Consider This
Most Americans have a mental picture of retirees and older people that is largely twenty years behind the times. Retirees are essentially disability–free and healthy for years into their 70's and beyond, particularly if they exercise, eat properly, remain active, and see their physician and dentist routinely, i.e. they can postpone or at least mitigate the effects of chronic illnesses and impairments.

"The body never lies."
Martha Graham, dancer, choreographer (1894-1991)

Obesity or excess body weight is a risk factor for coronary artery disease, certain types of cancers, diabetes, hypertension, and functional disability. Between 1988-94 and the latest research in 1999-2000, obesity increased dramatically among men 65 and older and among women aged 65 -74, according to the National Center for Health Statistics (NCHS). In men aged 65 -74, obesity increased to 33.4% from 24.1% and women showed an increase to 38.8% from 26.9%.

"I use the word 'fat.' I use that word because that's what people are: they're fat. They're not bulky; they're not large, chunky, hefty or plump. And they're not big-boned. Dinosaurs were big-boned. These people are not overweight: this term somehow implies there is some correct weight. There is no correct weight. Heavy is also a misleading term. An aircraft carrier is heavy; it's not fat. Only people are fat, and that's what fat people are! They're fat!"
George Carlin, Grammy award winner, American stand-up comedian,
actor, author (1937--2008)

The prevalence of hypertension increases with age, especially for women over age 75 (85% for women over aged 75 and 71% in men over that age have hypertension.) Conversely, the prevalence of coronary heart disease and stroke was highest among older men. Diabetes also can have an early onset. 15.1% of men and 13% of women 65 and older have this illness. The message is clear…your ancestry and genes affect your health in aging, but exercise and diet can also impact one's future health and lifestyle.

Eating healthy is the diet that works

The research is irrefutable: The type and amount of food you eat matters. Good nutrition can help lower your risk of developing certain diseases such as cancer, heart disease, and diabetes, as well as energize you, help you fight stress, and help you maintain a healthy weight.

Of course, there's plenty of conflicting advice on the "best" diet. One place to start is www.MyPyramid.gov, the U.S. Department of Agriculture website describing the current food pyramid and including the latest medical research as well as recommendations that are a little different from what your mother thought was good for you. Living with the pyramid as a guide, you will probably be eating more fruit and vegetables and more whole grains, and finding ways to include omega-3 oil in your diet – for starters.

TIPS

While a healthy diet can provide most of the nutrients you need, you also may want to improve health or help relieve pain by taking vitamins or other supplements such as chondroitin, glucosamine, antioxidants (like vitamin C, grape seed extract, selenium), or the many others that crowd the shelves of supermarkets and pharmacies. Be sure to keep your doctor informed about any vitamins and supplements you use to avoid unintended interactions with prescription drugs.

Finally, probably most of us are familiar with the myriad of professional organizations in the market that assist individuals in taking control of their food intake. Some provide pre-measured food, others don't, but all serve a healthy dose of advice, attempts at motivating individuals to "do the right thing" orchestrate a regimen that can be followed, and when needed, provide counsel. The largest of these firms can be found on the Internet and are usually easily accessible. To begin a process that you can follow and be successful in following, contact Weight Watchers at www.weightwatchers.com, NutriSystems at www.nutrisystems.com , Jenny Craig at www.jennycraig.com , or Seattle Sutton at www.seattlesutton.com .

If you want to keep a full smile… Floss only the teeth you want to save and see your dentist twice annually

The caption above tells the key points that need to be made. Avoid dentures if you can…also avoid bridges and implants. Given the choice, seeing your dentist twice annually is a visit that should not be avoided. As was stated in a famous car repair advertisement, "Pay now or pay later"…and that point does not cover the pain (literally) when trouble flares up.

Medicare does not cover dental visits, nor do Medicare supplemental plans. Try not to postpone these visits. One needs to purchase separate coverage for dental, but often coverage is not worth much in savings. Most dentists understand this issue and will negotiate a reduced rate on dental services. There are also clinics that can provide "special or emergency services" for free or at reduced fees.

You can Google the American Dental Association for advice. They have a site titled "Oral Changes with Age" which answers frequently asked questions like: "What is dentistry doing to better serve older adults?", "Why do my teeth seem darker?" or "What should I know about implants?"

"What did you say?"… "Oh, I can see you now."

Again, there appears to be a misconception about sensory impairments with respect to retirees. Most think that the elderly cannot hear or see well. Not so. They can for the most part. Studies show that only about 3.1% of those 65-74 and 8.3% of those 75 and older had a hearing or vision-related limitation of activities. Prescription glasses or contact lenses normally address whatever problems exist. Cataracts also can be easily repaired via surgery.

Hearing loss existed for a third of non-institutionalized people aged 70 and older and in half the population 85 and older. Unfortunately, seniors are less likely to have hearing evaluations and use hearing aids than to have vision evaluations and to wear glasses.

You may be wondering, why include these statistics when the subject is retirement. In answer to this question, only one point needs to be made. Sensory issues may begin years before retirement and many Boomers and other pre-retirement individuals rarely see an Ophthalmologist or a hearing specialist as they are: 1) viewed as unnecessary, because no problem is observed; or 2) they are viewed as an expensive expenditure. It is beneficial to see a specialist at least once and take a hearing and eye examination. Get a record so you have a baseline for future year comparisons. You will not be sorry you took this step for future analysis or should changes occur.

"The joy of sex", you say.

Yes. The topic is sex. According to www.yahoo.com's encyclopedia "On Health: Sexuality and Physical Changes with Age", "The joy in sex and loving knows no age barriers. Almost everyone has the capacity to find lifelong pleasure in sex. To believe in the myth that older people have no interest in sex is to miss out on wonderful possibilities. Of course, being single through choice, divorce, or widowhood can present a problem and the number to choose from in your age group decreases." Still, it is recommended to pursue your objectives…it has been proven time and again…possibilities do exist for one who perseveres. The choice is yours: Whether it involves intimacy or sexuality or simply friendship, you decide what is important to you.

What to discuss with your spouse, partner, or your "significant other"

 After you retire, if not now, it is generally advisable that someone whom you trust (your spouse, partner, or a "significant other" like an adult child or a friend) be familiar with your health condition, and be available to be of assistance if you need it. And this commentary covers more than just emergencies. Not that you need to discuss all your ailments or the prescription drugs you may be taking, but you might wish to document them and put them in a place (along with a medical power of attorney and living will) where they can easily be found, if needed. In **Exercise 3 (page 92)**, "What To Discuss with Your Spouse, Partner, or Significant Other", thought-starters are presented for your further consideration along similar lines.

If you examined Exercise 3, did you find that you currently have thought through the various points presented? Are matters well in hand or are there points you might consider changing or following up on? How do you envision that retirement would change these considerations? Are there behaviors or practices that you or your significant other should change to live a healthier lifestyle? Could you act as a team and support one another toward establishing a healthier lifestyle? For example, do either of you still smoke?

The Surgeon-General is right

Death rates from heart disease are declining for the population 65 and older. While lung cancer has declined among men 65 to 85, it has increased among older women in all older age groups, surpassing breast cancer as the leading cause of cancer death.

If you smoke, there's no better time than now to quit. Using tobacco increases your risk of heart disease and cancer, and is responsible for one out of every five deaths in the United States, according to American Cancer Society estimates. The good news is that when you stop smoking, no matter how old you are, you experience major and immediate health benefits.

A healthy body needs a healthy mind

A series of studies appears to demonstrate that people who are at least mildly active through middle age and beyond are at about half the risk of dementia and Alzheimer's as inactive adults. (Source: www.seniorjournal.com)

Another myth...Dementia and Alzheimer's disease are a normal part of aging

Did You Know?

Dementia and Alzheimer's disease, both resulting in the irreversible deterioration of intellectual ability accompanied by emotional disturbances, are <u>not</u> seen in the vast majority of the elderly. According to the American Psychological Association, dementia affects between 5 and 7 percent of adults over age 65 and 30% of those over age 85.

Alzheimer's disease (AD) also is <u>not</u> a normal part of aging. Relatively few individuals as a percentage develop the disease. In 2000 according to the National Institutes of Health, 4.5 million people have the disease representing 7% in the 65-75 age group, (only 20% of these cases were considered severe), 53% were aged 75-85 and 40% were aged 80+. It is true that for every 5 years of aging beyond age 65, one's chance of developing the disease doubles. People with AD live an average 8-10 years with the disease and the average life-time cost per patient was $174,000 in a 2002 National Institute on Aging (NIA) study. To protect oneself against a possible financial burden such as this that could deplete one's retirement assets, many individuals choose to purchase long-term care insurance to avoid such an occurrence.

Should you have an interest in purchasing long-term care insurance, this may be a good time to contemplate the benefits of such a purchase. The earlier you purchase such insurance, the lower the premiums and there are fewer physical requirements. A number of insurance providers have agents who specialize specifically and exclusively on long-term care insurance.

Optimism drives results

"We plant seeds that will flower as results in our lives, so best to remove the weeds of anger, avarice, envy and doubt..."
Dorothy Day, Founder of the Catholic Worker Movement (1894-1980)

In many ways, maintaining your mental health is similar to keeping your physical ability sharp – use it or lose it. Optimism, learning new things, staying connected to others, and humor, are all components of good mental health. Increasingly, research supports the belief that maintaining a high level of physical activity, continuing to seek challenges in work and leisure, and being involved in social situations may actually provide protection against diseases like Alzheimer's.

"I am an optimist. It does not seem too much use being anything else."
Winston Churchill, Knighted British Parliamentarian, Minister of Defense during WWII,
Prime Minister (1874-1965)

Optimism involves both planning the future hopefully and finding satisfaction in each day. Finding mentally challenging activities, such as learning a language, blogging, or using all the features on your cell phone may be helping your brain to build new connections and pathways. This isn't a "smart pill" but a way of warding off age-related declines like memory loss. Whatever you're curious about or have always wanted to learn offers an opportunity to exercise your brain in a way that will pay mental fitness dividends.

In the chapter, "Time To Do Good and For Good Times," you are offered the opportunity to further examine the issue of developing Life-long Learning activities. You are also provided with two exercises called "Gaining Knowledge and Education: What Would I Like To Learn?" and "Pursuing Additional Formal Education" to further plan your areas of interest.

TIPS Participating in a regular social activity that keeps you connected to other people, like a book discussion club or a monthly neighborhood luncheon or card game, also seems to have a positive impact on brain function. In addition, current research suggests that humor will help you do more than exercise your smile muscles. Understanding a one-liner or cartoon can involve left and right brain connections, with your left brain understanding the words in a rational way, and your right brain discovering what's funny and rewarding you with laughter when you get the joke. Although there's more research to be done, scientists believe enjoying complex humor helps you make better social decisions, improves your memory, and increases creativity. Scientific studies now demonstrate the plasticity of the brain, which means that we can continue to expand our mental capabilities by exercising our brain and building new pathways. Just as with exercising a muscle, exercising the brain by learning new things can build more capacity and greater brain strength.

No joke – humor may help keep your memory sharp.

Good health delivers financial rewards:

When you eat well and exercise regularly, you not only feel better and increase your ability to enjoy life fully – you can also reap financial dividends. And money that you don't have to spend on health care is money that you can spend on living the retirement lifestyle you choose.

- Staying healthy will most likely keep you out of a nursing home longer. Most good nursing homes cost about $7,000 a month. The longer you avoid nursing home care, the more money in your pocket.
- Being overweight can cause serious illnesses such as diabetes. The money you will save on prescription drugs to deal with diabetes is only matched by.
- Losing weight can also lower your blood pressure and cholesterol levels. This, in turn, will save you many dollars at the prescription drug counter.
- The more you can minimize the need for prescription drugs by staying healthy through physical activity and healthy eating, the better you will feel, the more serious illnesses you will avoid and the longer you will live and be able to enjoy the money you didn't have to spend on prescription drugs. Over the next 20 years, it is possible for a couple to spend about $70,000 on prescription drugs, in addition to the costs of over-the-counter drugs, dental care and long term care.

Exercise 4 (page 93), "Assessing Your Health and Dealing With Possible or Current Ailments, Illnesses and Medical Conditions" presented later in this chapter provides you with another opportunity to determine the future of your health-related activities and how you can deal with your current and projected ailments, illnesses, and medical conditions. Assuming you completed the exercise, now examine what has and has not worked for you, as well as what you think could work for you. Of course, thinking you can do something is a long way from actually doing it. Obviously, it very much depends on your commitment.

If you completed the assessment described immediately above, what did you discover about yourself? Did you have some new insights about your attitudes and intentions regarding your health?

Thus far, the emphasis has been placed primarily on your physical well-being. The text also mentioned your attitude. What about your spiritual side?

Spirituality

A holistic approach to health also encompasses a spiritual aspect. For many people, spiritual health depends on defining clear values, following your passions, and making a difference. Retirement is an ideal time to begin considering your legacy: What will you leave behind? Will you leave a mark? What have you done that says your life was meaningful?

Some psychiatrists have theorized that life happens in stages. Early stages are devoted to making a place in the world, getting an occupation, marrying, having children. In mid-life and our later years, we discover a need to turn "inward" and reconnect with aspects of ourselves (our "spiritual self") that we had to silence earlier when constructing our daily lives.

Typically at this stage, we increasingly pay attention to developing and nurturing our spirituality. It can become a time of transition toward understanding the importance of "who we are," not just "how we are perceived" (with its associated focus on money, power, and authority.) We need to ask the philosophical questions about the meaning and purpose of our lives, and try to answer the question, "Where do I fit in?" We need to deepen our relationship to our spiritual self, be it through a traditional religious faith or some other form of spiritual connection.

Consider This

We also may find ourselves focused on the opportunity to become a wiser person (some might say a sage.) This encompasses learning how to harvest the wisdom we developed through our maturity and transform it into a legacy for future generations. When we look back in our memories, we can often find pearls of wisdom to use as catalysts for more productive actions in the future.

We find that our ego needs for personal achievement and success diminish, and that we are better able to respond to the needs of our family, our community, and the nation. We become increasingly aware of the rewards of mentoring and giving to others, ultimately acting as "wisdom keepers and elders of the tribe."

A review of **Exercise 5 (page 97),** "Your Spiritual Health Check-up", can provide a deeper sense of how you could add more time and energy to this area of your life.

If you completed exercise 5, does it set you on a different course for taking on a new set of challenges in your life? If so, bravo for you!

Into every life, a little rain must fall

"Even too much sunshine can be devastating, while only with rain can growth occur. Accept both as part of the growing process in the garden of life."
Donald S. Neviaser, *The Inner View: Life Enhancing Perspectives*

It has been said many times that "change is inevitable and unchanging" and that part of life is the inevitability of surprise. Some call it fate; others call it by other names. Regardless, change and surprise by definition bring on stress, tension and the sense that we either need to take control or be controlled by circumstance. Certainly a little stress is said to be good…take sports competition or being pushed a little to get the best out of individuals and groups of people. On the other hand, too much stress may result in irritability, anger, depression or the use of drugs, alcohol, and overeating as coping mechanisms.

 Each person has to deal with stress and tension in their own way.   What about you?

Adults over 50, at some point have existential issues: fear of aging, fear of end of life, fear of being alone, fear of an incapacitating illness, etc. Without a forum to address these issues, people can easily have little energy or feel depressed and this may impact their physical health. There are resources to help in discussing and dealing with these issues, including counselors, mental health professionals, clergy, support groups, friends, and so forth. Since you are interested in having the best retirement possible, it is important to recognize that some of these issues may affect your mental health and it is important to recognize them so that they may be addressed.

"Stress is the trash of modern life - we all generate it, but if you don't dispose of it properly, it will pile up and overtake your life."
Danzae Pace, author of on-line blogging

In **Exercise 6 (page 98)**, "Retirement Stressors," and the last of the exercises in this chapter, you are given the opportunity to go through a list of what are considered the most prevalent stressors for the general population. Which apply to your circumstances? What do you think of your coping mechanisms for dealing with the ones that currently apply, and could apply to you in the years ahead as you plan your retirement? Are you in control or do circumstances control you? What needs to be done?

**"When you find yourself stressed, ask yourself one question:
Will this matter in 5 years from now?
If yes, then do something about the situation. If no, then let it go."**

Catherine Pulsifer, author, glass artist (1957--)

Please note that The RetireRight Center is also there to help. This <u>non-profit</u> consulting company in Chicago exists to provide training workshops and individualized coaching on the topic of transitioning into retirement. The RetireRight Center is available as an adjunct to doing the work of planning on your own. You can learn more about the Center at <u>www.retirerightcenter.org</u>.

CHAPTER 3

PATH 3: KEEPING IN SHAPE

EXERCISES

If you have not already done so, now is your opportunity to complete the following exercises which will assist you to understanding your commitment to future good health in retirement, thereby, hopefully helping you to consider dealing with alternative situations and opportunities.

Exercise 1: Where Are You Now, Where Are You Going?

Exercise 2: Excuses, Excuses, Excuses

Exercise 3: What to Discuss with Your Spouse, Partner, or Significant Other

Exercise 4: Assessing Your Health and Dealing with Possible or Current Ailments, Illnesses and Medical Conditions

Exercise 5: Your Spiritual Health Check-up

Exercise 6: Retirement Stressors

At the conclusion of the exercises is a "**Summary of Decisions**" page, which will allow you to think through some of the thoughts and ideas you have been gathering. Please take some time to evaluate the information you have reviewed and created, and then summarize some key points, in writing, that you would like to pursue in putting together your final action plan in this book's last chapter, "**Your Action Plan…Putting It All Together.**"

EXERCISE 1

WHERE ARE YOU NOW? WHERE ARE YOU GOING?

These questionnaires are designed to help you consider ways in which you can best care for your body, mind, and soul.

Mark the following True or False:

1. I have an annual physical every year with appropriate screenings.

2. My body weight is within range for height and frame type.

3. I visit my dentist for cleaning and screening every six months.

4. I practice good dental hygiene, including flossing.

5. I don't smoke and try to avoid second-hand smoke.

6. I get 7 or more hours of sleep each night.

7. I pay attention to advances in medical care, supplements, drugs, etc. so that I can be aware of changes that may impact my quality of life now and in the future.

8. My average daily use of alcohol is less than two oz. of liquor or 2 cans of beer per day.

9. Most days my diet includes: 5 servings fruit, 5 servings vegetables, 6 servings of wholegrain bread or pasta, low fat dairy foods, lean fish or poultry, nuts and seeds.

10. I limit caffeine by drinking no more than one cup coffee/tea or one can caffeinated soda each day.

11. Stress in my life is usually manageable.

12. Most days I get 30 minutes of aerobic exercise.

13. Strength training 3 days a week is part of my routine.

14. I do stretching exercises daily.

15. People are not surprised to hear that I'm learning something new, i.e., a sport, a language, a new game, how to trace my family's genealogy.

16. I have close friends and relationships and continue to meet new people and find new ways of interacting with others.

17. I spend most days involved in activities I look forward to and enjoy.

18. This questionnaire has given me several ideas for improving the quality of my physical, mental, social and/or spiritual health.

Tips for Following Up on Your Responses:

The above questions should give you some areas on which you can focus to improve your physical/mental/social health and your level of fitness. To those that you answered "**False**," this may be an opportunity for you to make further improvements to your health and fitness levels.

Questions 1-7 focus on basic habits for maintaining good health.

Questions 8-10 concern diet.

Question 11 is about stress management, which impacts health and fitness in a variety of ways.

Questions 12-14 are about the various types of exercise each of us needs to do to keep us as fit as possible.

Questions 15 and 16 focus on ways of maintaining social and mental health.

Question 17 is about having an optimistic, positive attitude.

Question 18 reflects your ability to identify positive changes that are available to you.

[Please return to page 76 to continue reading Chapter 3.]

EXERCISE 2

EXCUSES, EXCUSES, EXCUSES

Following are some reasons individuals give for not exercising or eating properly. Check off all quotes which apply to you:

1. "I don't have the time."
2. "I don't have the energy."
3. "I have a heart condition."
4. "I don't have the willpower."
5. "I love food."
6. "I don't know the calories."
7. "I can't control myself."
8. "I am always eating out, so I can't control what goes into the foods I am eating."
9. "I hate eating breakfast."
10. "I eat with my grandchildren, so I have to have junk food around for them."
11. "I don't do the shopping for the right foods."
12. "My family and I, and all my ancestors, have always been heavy."
13. "I don't have the space for exercise equipment."
14. "My exercise equipment is broken."
15. "It is hard to reserve tee/court time."
16. "Golf/tennis and similar sports are too expensive."
17. "Exercise is very time consuming."
18. "I have a physical ailment that prevents me from exercising."
19. "I lack the means or equipment to diet/exercise."
20. "I know what to eat in order to eat properly, I just eat too much of it."
21. "I injured myself so I can't exercise."
22. "I am afraid of hurting myself if I exercise."
23. "My husband (wife/partner) likes the way I look (heavy)."
24. "I am always hungry, and food is always around (e.g., the office, home, etc.)"
25. "I just love _____" (You fill in the food, e.g., chocolate.)

How many applied to you? Can you think of other comments like these?
Is it time to change your habits?

Examine what prevents you from doing the right thing. Can you start a new set of healthy habits? Identify what they would be:

New habit # 1:   New habit # 2:

How could you build your new habits into your daily routine? Could you commit to doing this by telling someone else about your intention asking them to monitor your commitment?

[Please return to page 77 to continue reading Chapter 3.]

EXERCISE 3

WHAT TO DISCUSS WITH
YOUR SPOUSE, PARTNER, OR SIGNIFICANT OTHER

1. Have I made my goals known to my spouse, partner, significant-other, close friend or relative, regarding living a healthier lifestyle through exercise and a healthy diet? Have I discussed our working together toward attaining these goals?

2. Is the person mentioned above, also in need of changing their behavior in some way to achieve a healthier lifestyle? Can you assist them toward this healthier lifestyle or become partners around common goals?

3. How will these topics be affected by retirement?

4. Have you and the person you identified in this exercise discussed:
    *   what to do in case of medical emergency?
    *   where you keep your documents relating to your prescribed medicines, and other documents relating to medical and legal actions?
    *   your whereabouts and plans in the event of changing circumstances?

Based on the above discussion:

1. Do you need to do anything that currently is not in good order?

2. Would retirement or retirement planning affect these matters?

[Please return to page 81 to continue reading Chapter 3.]

EXERCISE 4

ASSESSING YOUR HEALTH AND DEALING WITH POSSIBLE OR CURRENT AILMENTS, ILLNESSES AND MEDICAL CONDITIONS

Health assessment

A. To what extent do I agree or disagree with the following statements?

I see myself:	Strongly Disagree	Somewhat Disagree	Somewhat Agree	Strongly Agree
Relocating to a warm climate				
Walking 10,000 steps a day				
Lifting weights 3 times a week				
Being enrolled in a health club				
Exercising 3 times a week				
Going on a diet or avoiding eating too many calories				
Eating healthy foods				
Smiling a lot				
Reading about good health or healthy habits				
Stretching daily				
Getting 8 hours sleep				
Participating in occasional recreational exercise				
Participating in occasional sports				

B. What do my answers tell me about myself? Am I pleased with my profile? (Note: the more "somewhat agrees" and "strongly agrees" I have, the more likely my routine will support a healthy lifestyle.)

II. Ailments and what to do to mitigate them in retirement

There are costs associated with the ailments and illnesses that you have…not only the cost of prescription medicines, but also the limitations that are placed on your ability to do the fulfilling activities you value in retirement.

Now evaluate what ailments, illnesses, and conditions you face and examine how serious they are. Ask yourself: what can be done about them? What have you tried? What are the chances for improvement? What are the costs? These questions may help you take a look at how exercise can help mitigate the costs that health barriers pose to a fulfilling lifestyle.

Complete the chart and the additional questions. In the first column list your ailments/sicknesses, illnesses, and conditions. In the second column identify how limiting they are to your lifestyle in retirement, and their actual monetary cost:

Ailment, Illness, Condition	How Limiting to Lifestyle	Estimated Monetary Costs

1. List your efforts to minimize or eliminate those physical conditions listed above. What have you tried?

2. Based on what you tried to do, what were the results?

3. Based on the results that ensued, to what extent can you honestly be successful in minimizing or virtually eliminating your physical conditions?

Examples of exercises:

- Walking 10,000 steps a day
- Lifting weights 3 times a week
- Stretching daily
- Playing tennis
- Playing golf
- Playing shuffleboard or a less rigorous competitive sport
- Swimming 3 times a week
- Running
- Tossing a ball
- Bicycling or using a stationary bicycle
- Getting on a treadmill daily or three times a week
- Using an elliptical machine
- Yoga
- Aerobics or calisthenics
- Others of your choosing, perhaps at a health club

Complete this chart using the list of exercises above.

What I should ideally be doing	What I could realistically do	What I honestly already do	What I view as a gap that I should address

III. A. Examine the activities listed above.

- Check off which you believe will help you feel better, or alleviate or minimize your conditions?
- Which would you be willing to start or increase?
- Which would be easily adoptable or could be integrated into your lifestyle?
- Which could be fun to do?
- Is there a friend you can do it with? This may make it more enjoyable or "nudge" or motivate you to follow through when your motivation ebbs from time-to-time?

Remember to start with an examination from your physician to make sure you are in condition to take on more exercise. Then begin simply with a walk around the block, for example, and move on from there. No need to run a marathon when you have been inactive for a long time.

B. Examine your daily schedule.

- Would you be willing to commit to specific times to follow up on the activities above?
- Write your commitment below and make a note to add it to your Action Plan (page 238) and also to your daily calendar.

[Please return to page 84 to continue reading Chapter 3.]

EXERCISE 5

YOUR SPIRITUAL HEALTH CHECK-UP

Each of us has to address the future in our own unique way. What we need to ask ourselves is:

1. What have I contributed to improving the world?

2. How do I feel about my contributions?

3. Do I feel complete and whole from a spiritual perspective?

4. If not, what do I need to do?

[Please return to page 85 to continue reading Chapter 3.]

EXERCISE 6

RETIREMENT STRESSORS

Life changes are always difficult and entering retirement is no different. For many of us it is an opportunity to fulfill our dreams, i.e. it is a time to have the freedom to choose what we wish to do with our time. We get a measure of freedom to make decisions about how we will structure our time, who we wish to spend time with, what we wish to create or do, how and where we will spend our money, and so forth.

Conversely, there will be obstacles for many of us as well; obstacles such as insufficient savings; declining health; adult dependent children issues; elderly dependent parents: distance from immediate families, others pleading for our time or money, and so forth.

Often Boomers and others avoid the effort of projecting or envisioning themselves transitioning into retirement because of the negative potential difficulties they assume will be encountered (see list below.) Simply put, these are stressors they would prefer not dwelling upon. The consequences of this avoidance only exacerbates the probability that if these circumstances occur, we will be <u>less prepared to deal with them</u>.

Confronting Our Fears

This exercise could be very helpful to you. If you take time to complete it, you will be greatly enriched by knowing that you can both identify stressors and then take CONTROL in order to address obstacles now or in the future.

This exercise is in three parts:
- First, the exercise asks you to identify the stressors in your life by examining the sample list of changes that occur in a person's life.
- Second, it asks you to complete the second column by rating your stress level.
- Third, you are asked to rate the stressors you could conceivably face in your later years, i.e. you will be doing these ratings based on your assumptions about future stressors. Remember that you are speculating… no one has a crystal ball to know what we will need to address in future years. For now, "just run" with this exercise as an opportunity to see how you could deal with possible changes in the future.
- Also consider that every situation ultimately can be mitigated or solved if you recognize it for what it is, a change that provides for greater learning and action.

To a large extent, the items listed in this exercise are rank-ordered based on the extent stress researchers have found provide the greatest stress to individuals. The list is based on research from Drs. Thomas Holmes and Richard Rahe, who theorized that it is the amount of change required by an event, rather than change itself that causes ill health tied to stress. They found that Stressful Life Events can be both "positive" and "negative", but both types can contribute to stress, elevated blood pressure, increases in adrenaline, reduced immune system functioning, and long-term heart disease.

Outward manifestations and warning signs of high levels of stress include:

- Extreme or chronic fatigue
- Frequent colds and headaches
- Persistent stomach aches or bowel problems
- Reoccurring tension headaches
- Repeated minor accidents attributable to loss of concentration
- Reoccurring skin problems
- Depression, or a constant lack of feeling comfortable or secure
- Inability to sleep

Determine the amount of stress in your life today and what you anticipate in retirement. Assign each item a rating number 0 to 4:

0 = Not an issue
1= An unlikely issue
2 = Is a slight issue
3 = Is definitely an issue
4 = Is definitely a big issue

Change Events	**Current Ratings**	**Later Years' Ratings (anticipated)**
Death of a spouse		
Divorce		
Marital Separation		
Jail/Institution detention		
Close family member's death		
Major personal injury		
Marriage		
Being fired from work		
Marital reconciliation		
Retirement from work		
Behavior/health change in family		
Sexual difficulties		
A birth, adoption, child moves in		
Bankruptcy		
Major financial change		
Death of a close friend		
Taking out a new major loan		
Changing sleep habits		
Foreclosure on loan		
In-law troubles		
Spouse begins/ends working		
Moving		
Illness of spouse or loved one		

Change Events	Current Ratings	Later Years' Ratings (anticipated)
Becoming a caregiver		
Care of aging parent		
Parent moves in		
Sleep problems		
	Total:	Total:

Rating scale: Above 35: Reasonably high stress level; 20-34: Moderate stress level; Below 20: Low stress level

Having completed the previous exercise on Retirement Stressors and examined the results of your ratings, you can now respond to the following set of questions which ask you for specific actions that you can take to address or reduce the stressors in your life.

1. To the extent possible, what might I be able to do about the primary stressors that exist in my life today and which I identified in the above exercise?

2. Who can I turn to for help or support in beginning to address or to control the stressors in my life?

3. Anticipating future retirement, what can I do to reduce anticipated stressors before they become a reality?

[Please return to page 86 to continue reading Chapter 3.]

> For even more help and experienced people to talk to who are trained in retirement planning, please call the **RetireRight Center** for an appointment to meet with someone, either on the phone or in person. **312-673-3842** or www.retirerightcenter.org .

SUMMARY OF DECISIONS

PATH 3: KEEPING IN SHAPE

Now that you have some background on the topic of "**Keeping In Shape**" and have completed the exercises in this chapter, you should have reached some personal decisions which will later become **key (critical) inputs toward completing your final Action Plan in Chapter 8.** Think about what you would like **to do more of,** or perhaps, what you would like to **do less of** in preparing for your most realistic and fulfilling retirement. Consider in what capacity you see yourself changing your lifestyle and actions in the future and why.

 What do I want to commit to working on related to my vision of a successful
You   retirement?
Decide

1. I would like to continue to examine taking specific actions to improve my chances for continued good health.

2. I would like to continue building on the information borne out by research on how healthy aging is largely a product of what I do, i.e. it is much more than genetics.

3. I would like to go on the internet and through other sources as well, continue my health self-assessment, thereby continuing to build a healthy physical and mental style of living that will be helpful for my remaining years in retirement.

4. I would like to commit toward visiting with my key physicians annually to ensure I receive their sage advice; I will also plan to listen to their advice relating to trying to maintain a healthy lifestyle.

What are your **key decisions?**

Key Decision A

_____

_____

Key Decision B

_____

_____

Key Decision C

_____

_____

Other thoughts, questions, ideas, research that needs to be done, etc.:

Please transfer your decisions into Chapter 8 (Page 229): "Your Action Plan."

CHAPTER 4

PATH 4: BEING AT HOME

"At a certain season of our life we are accustomed to consider every spot as the possible site of a house."
Henry David Thoreau, *Where I Lived, and What I Lived For*

In this chapter, you will have the opportunity to:

1. Explore what qualities make a house and a community your home.
2. Examine the factors that will influence the type of housing which you may choose now and in the future.
3. Consider relocation options and examine your reasons for choosing to relocate.

What makes housing your home?

Your housing means much more than something to keep out the rain and the cold. What is home to you? For most people, home means friends; community; and a lifetime of memories. As you progress into the next stage of life, there are many things to consider in terms of living arrangements.

The house you are living in is full of memories of your family, friends and your younger years. But will this same house accommodate your changing needs? Renovation may be the answer to staying in your current home, allowing you to adjust the physical characteristics of the house to make it easier to get around when the need arises. However, if your income is limited, your current home may be too costly.

According to a recent study by Home Depot, more than 60% of Boomers plan to stay in their current homes for at least the next 5 years. And 65% of those Boomers plan to remodel or make improvements to their homes. The trend is to stay put and modify their homes to accommodate future physical needs.

Consider This

In response to this trend, remodelers are becoming certified aging-in-place specialists (CAPS). These building contractors and other professionals in related areas of expertise are receiving specialized training to help them understand the needs of an aging population and how to cater to this group and their particular style.

You may decide that you would like to move closer to your children and grandchildren. Or you may want to move to a warmer climate. Senior style communities are often appealing to those who want to be surrounded by other seniors and where numerous amenities and activities, as well as medical assistance, are close at hand. Safety of the neighborhood is also to be considered. You may also want to make sure that medical facilities, shopping, and public transportation are available in the location you select.

To get you started on thinking through various factors in choosing a house and where to live, please respond to the questions in **Exercise 1 (page 115),** "Decisions, Decisions, Decisions."

Now that you have pondered the questions in Exercise 1 and have discussed the responses with those people who are closest to you, have you been able to clarify your thinking a bit on this subject?

"Home is Where the Heart Is and Hence a Movable Feast."
Angela Carter, English novelist and journalist (1940-1992)

**"Mid pleasures and palaces though we may roam,
Be it ever so humble, there's no place like home."**
John Howard Payne, American actor, author and singer (1791-1852)

Thinking about relocating?

You
Decide

Remember that housing and location are two separate considerations in determining where to live. You will need to gather information from many sources to provide a broad base for your decisions. The primary consideration should be the way you choose to live. Visualize your desired lifestyle for the next 10 years. Recognizing that there is no "utopia," take time to assess the tangible and intangible elements that create that special place for you.

If you're considering relocating, think carefully about the many geographic areas available to you and consider the lifestyle in those places. It may be helpful to list specific cities, states and/or regions in order of your preference and comment on why each of those places appeals to you.

It may be fun for you to look at **Exercise 2 (page 117),** "Prioritizing Your Options" and begin to contemplate various locations and types of environments.

In completing Exercise 2, did you have any Ah-Ha's? Any surprises or awakenings? Did you dream of moving to the mountains and your spouse has always wanted to live near the ocean? Did you want to live in a rural setting and your children live in big cities? These are important considerations in your planning process that need to be discussed and reconciled.

How is your budget for relocating?

As is evident from other chapters of this book, most Americans are not saving enough for retirement. If this is the case for you, it would behoove you to search for a retirement location where property taxes, and, perhaps, sales taxes, are lower. Then too, you may choose to downsize your current home and reduce maintenance expenses, as well as the higher property taxes. In your budgeting for relocation, do also think about your moving expenses and factor that into your change of residence.

> Some websites that may prove useful in identifying locations with lower housing prices and tax benefits are: www.findyourspot.com; www.neighborhoodscout.com; and www.bestplaces.net.

Relocating is not always easy, which is why the Census Bureau reported that only about 7% of people over 50 moved to another locale. In making your decision about moving, it is wise to consider items such as availability of health care, shopping, museums, cultural attractions, sports activities, access to airports, weather patterns and other amenities that are important to your lifestyle. Will you be far from friends and family, especially in times when you may need assistance? Is there an educational institution nearby that would provide educational and cultural events? If you need or want to continue working, are there opportunities to work in the area you are considering?

In short, there are many things to contemplate if you are trying to decide whether to move to another part of the country or the world. But if you have a dream or a wish that you want to pursue, do try it out first. Don't make any major commitment until you are very sure that this is the right move for you. Many people have moved to a vacation spot they loved and realized, all too late, that this location was great for a vacation, but not as a permanent residence.

Rule of Thumb

The **rule of thumb** here is to rent in that dream location for a year or more to be sure it is right for you. After living in that place in every season and seeing whether you like the climate, the people and the amenities, as well as checking out availability of housing and cost of living, you will be in a much better position to make your decision.

In **Exercise 3 (page 118)**, "Exploring Relocation," you will have the opportunity to compare your current housing location with other options you may have in mind. The rating scale will allow you to compare numerically several options. Do have fun with that and come back when you have finished.

Now that you have had the chance to compare various locations where you might choose to live in Exercise 3, did you make any discoveries or learn something new about each of your options?

"Home is not where you live, but where they understand you."
Christian Morganstern, poet

There may be challenges to your desire to relocate. These include:
- Your spouse or partner doesn't want to move.
- Your spouse or partner is still very involved in his/her own career.
- You have children who need or want you to stay close to them.
- You have an aging parent who needs your support.
- You are committed to social and cultural activities in your community.
- The costs of moving, including capital gains taxes on the sale of your current home, moving costs, re-doing a new home, etc.

As stated earlier, it is important to take time to really get to know another location before making your decision to make a change. Even if it's just the other side of town, talk to people who live there. Ask all your questions. Try and rent for several months in that area. See if it appeals to you on a day-to-day basis. And, especially, if you're planning to move to another city or region, live there for a year on a trial basis and learn what it's like in that area. If you've vacationed in a particular area, try and live there during a non-vacation season.

Be smart! Before you make a major move, make many telephone calls and talk to others who live in the location in which you are interested. "Google" their site, and follow up with personal visits to their grocery stores, your future house of worship, movie theaters, their hospital complex, libraries, local educational institutions and other local attractions that would interest you. Test out driving distances and traffic patterns. Do your research, but understand that nothing replaces first-hand experience over time to the "real world" that exists there.

Living Abroad

Avoid the pain of a couple who moved permanently to southern France – without trying it out. It sounded like a dream come true. They sold their home, packed up everything and moved. A year later they returned to their former city. When their old friends asked them what happened, they replied that they had failed retirement. They missed their friends. They were too far away from their children and grandchildren. They felt like foreigners (which they were!) They never got comfortable with the different way of life that they encountered there.

There are all sorts of house swaps that you could try before moving permanently. Or, you could rent out your house and use the rental fee to pay for living in another locale for a year. You can Google "house swaps" to get started. There are many websites that deal with home exchanges around the globe.

So, how much housing can you afford?

Rule of Thumb

There are many differing **"Rules of Thumb"** out there that purvey advice to homebuyers. A "rule of thumb" is meant to be a greatly simplified estimate for a complicated matter. For example, the Northwest Community Credit Union says 1.5 times your gross annual income would be a good estimate for how much you can afford to spend on a house. CNN Money says 2.5 times. Washington Mutual Bank suggests anywhere from 3 to 5 times. As a broad generalization, most people can afford to purchase a house worth about three times their total (gross) annual income, assuming a 20% down payment and a moderate amount of other long-term debts, such as car payments. With no other debts, you can probably afford a house worth up to four or even five times your annual income. Most people estimate that housing should cost 25% to 30% of one's income.

For retirees, the picture may be very different, as retirees frequently own their current homes and have paid up their mortgages. In selling their current home, they would be able to afford to pay a similar amount or less for a new home and not have to take out a mortgage. This would help with cash flow. Whether you choose to borrow on your home or take out a new mortgage would be a good discussion to have with your financial advisor.

Just to get the feel for how other housing options compare with your own home, turn to, **Exercise 4 (Page 120),** "Comparing Housing," see how your current dwelling stacks up.

After completing Exercise 4, what did you learn about your own house as compared with other living arrangements? Did this make you more or less satisfied with the status quo?

Fitness at Home

"Lack of activity destroys the good condition of every human being, while movement and methodical physical exercise save it and preserve it."
Plato, 424-348 BC, Athens, Greece, Philosopher, mathematician, writer

Many retirement communities are attracting residents with facilities that promote exercise and interesting athletic activities. Fitness centers have become the norm and locations which include ski resorts and hiking trails are very popular. Facilities with trainers and wellness programs are also in demand. Boomers not only want to live longer, they want to prevent age-related diseases and avoid illnesses that will slow them down and cause them to change their lifestyle. Exercise is definitely the key to slowing the aging process and, fortunately, Boomers are accustomed to an active lifestyle. As the population ages, the US Census Bureau predicts that the costs of caring for these individuals will create a large burden on the nation's health care bill. As if we needed another reason to stay healthy, avoiding enormous health care bills is right up there.

Thinking Ahead

Some of the factors most important in considering your future housing needs include: cost, location, size, level of independence and proximity to friends and family. Depending on how these factors influence their decisions, retirees choose from a variety of housing options:
- If they are healthy enough to care for themselves, most retirees choose to live at home. Sometimes, they need extra help from a caregiver or a family member who may come in to assist.
- Some retirees live with family members, especially as they become less independent.
- Assisted living or retirement communities offer additional care, such as personal care and medical care.
- Other retirement communities also have nursing facilities, when the need arises.
- Nursing homes provide medical care when people can no longer live independently.

Most people want to stay where they are as long as possible. This raises the feasibility of adapting your current residence for future needs, when and if necessary. So, if you're remodeling or building new, incorporate as many "Aging-in-Place" designs into your home as possible, such as showers with flat entrances, room for wheelchairs, low cabinets, no front steps, and a bedroom on the first floor. Don't forget that coping with stairs may become a challenge in later years.

In evaluating your current housing, there are many factors to consider. Please turn to **Exercise 5 (page 122),** "Evaluating Your Current Housing," to begin the process of assessing how well your current housing will meet your future needs.

Now that you have answered the questions in Exercise 5, did you determine how well your current housing meets your needs now and in the future? If you are not sure about this, how will you find out more information?

With the large influx of Boomers into the aging marketplace, more and more people are becoming consultants to this age group, from handymen to accountants to home care specialists. As well as a welcome avenue of future employment for retiring individuals, those needing assistance will be able to call on a larger and growing pool of available resources to help with life's little challenges.

The four physical life cycle periods

As you grow older, you may transition through four distinct life cycle periods tied to your physical ability to perform key life-maintenance functions. For each period, you may wish to consider specifically where you would wish to reside. Some individuals choose to move to a single facility that will accommodate their changing needs, namely, the transition from independent living to assisted living to skilled nursing care. Others strongly prefer not to follow such a plan.

 Think about what housing or residence you would desire or require in each of the following periods:

Consider This

1. Upon retirement...assumes good physical health.
2. If the quality of your health begins to deteriorate (i.e. when you lack the energy or physical means or stamina), but have the ability to do virtually all that living independently requires.
3. If you begin to need assistance with certain life activities like grocery shopping, doing laundry, house cleaning or house maintenance, visiting friends or your doctors, preparing meals, etc.
4. If you require assistance with at least one of life's basic routines like getting dressed, eating meals, bathing, using a rest room, moving about, etc.

This may be the time to consider Long-Term Care insurance. Do discuss the benefits and costs of this type of insurance with your financial advisor or an expert in the LTC insurance field.

Boomers on the move:

William Frey, a demographer with the Brookings Institute and the University of Michigan says that today's retirement choices are university towns, resort destinations and suburban oases on the outskirts of major cities. The cultural advantages of these locations are a big draw. Geographic assets would include national parks, outdoor activities and beautiful scenery. More than anything else, retirees don't want to be bored. This generation of boomers wants to keep up the active lifestyle they have developed in their earlier years. Besides the physical challenges of golf courses and tennis courts, retirees are attracted to art and photography classes, courses at the colleges and concert venues. People want to maintain their lively and recreational lifestyle. They don't want to just graduate to a rocking chair in their retirement years.

 Beyond the lifestyle concerns, if income is an issue and retirees want to relocate, they are choosing locations where local taxes are less than their present home. Some states have no personal income tax. Others have lower property taxes. If this is something that would interest you, you can search for such locales through

Consider
This
AARP and in various retirement guides, such as *Retirement Places Rated.*

Another creative approach to housing involves shared housing. Some people are finding it comfortable and cost effective to share a home with one or two other people. It would be wise to get to know these people before you make a permanent arrangement and be sure to have enough space so that each person can be alone if they choose to do so.

Some retirement communities feature intergenerational housing so that young families can have the benefit of mingling with experienced members of the community. This is especially salubrious when very young children and older adults share projects together.

?

Did You Know? Our research has shown that, even though many Boomers can afford to move, most of them are staying in their current location. This may have to do with proximity to family and the comfort of a familiar environment. Most are considering frequent travel, rather than relocation. Then too, even though many boomers have enough financial resources to retire, they are choosing to continue to work, either full time or part time, or move into new work-related activities, such as consulting. Since it is becoming easier to find occupations that allow one to work from home, the desire to move is diminishing. Those who find that their finances in retirement will not keep pace with their expenditures will need to continue to work and need to be in a location where jobs are available. For all these reasons, retirees may choose to continue to live in the same location, and even in the same house, as the years go by.

From the beginning, the Boomer population has been setting trends. This will also be true as they move into their retirement years. This may mean that they will swell the ranks of volunteers as Marc Freedman described in his book *Prime Time.* There may also be large shifts of population into communities which are attractive to retirees. If you are among this group, you have already experienced the energy that comes with large masses of people choosing the same activities at the same time. On the other hand, if you are planning to relocate, you may need to be aware of this surge and make your move before the crowd does.

Retirement is an exciting time to fulfill your dreams by choosing your location and housing arrangements so you can hopefully:

- Avoid all that home maintenance work;
- Travel easily without having to worry about your place;
- Enjoy the weather conditions throughout the year;
- Use your home as a locale to participate in the activities you most want to have in the forefront of your life;
- Have the ability to easily invite your friends or grandchildren over for a visit;
- Participate in sporting events like golf, or as a spectator either in person or in front of your TV;
- Work out with friends or at a fitness center;
- Do the gardening that you love, or use that beautiful kitchen, or have that sunny room with the perfect light to paint, or go into that dark room you had built for developing your photographs;
- Attend those community or church meetings you enjoy;
- Sit in on those nearby university or other educational courses that you always wanted to attend;
- Simply relax and take naps in that cozy place of yours;
- Commute a reasonable distance to work or to volunteer;
- Have a home office to start a new business;
- Work part time.

You get the idea. You earned it in retirement...it's your time to enjoy it! Make your home your place to "nest," entertain, or whatever. Only you can decide what to do to make it happen!

CHAPTER 4

PATH 4: BEING AT HOME

EXERCISES

If you have not already done so, now is your opportunity to complete the following exercises which will assist you in making decisions related to examining the type of community, housing, and location you would like to live in the future, thereby, hopefully helping you to consider dealing with alternative situations and opportunities.

·

Exercise 1:   Decisions, Decisions, Decisions

Exercise 2:   Prioritizing Your Options

Exercise 3:   Exploring Relocation

Exercise 4:   Comparing Housing

Exercise 5:   Evaluating Your Current Housing

At the conclusion of the exercises is a "**Summary of Decisions**" page, which will allow you to think through some of the thoughts and ideas you have been gathering in completing this chapter. Please take some time to evaluate the information you have both reviewed and created, and then summarize some key points in writing that you would like to pursue in putting together your final action plan in this book's last chapter, "**Your Action Plan...Putting It All Together**".

EXERCISE 1

DECISIONS, DECISIONS, DECISIONS

Deciding on a location and the type of housing that you desire and can afford are key decisions. Answer the following questions and then discuss your answers with those closest to you to help you with your planning process.

1. How would you describe the current financial condition of your current residence, i.e. live in a fully paid off house valued at $_____, our home is in need of repair to the tune of $_____, we rent, our townhouse maintenance of $_____ is going up dramatically each year, etc.

2. My key family members live (close, far) _____ and how do I feel about this in my retirement years? Do actions need to be taken relating to this?

3. What do I think about our local climate? How about a love for water or other physical environmental conditions, i.e. mountains, a rural setting, suburbia, the city lifestyle? Any concerns that would need to be addressed?

4. What do I think about local hospitals and health care facilities? Need top rated care facilities be nearby?

5. To what extent do I want to be actively working or volunteering in some capacity and will my retirement community provide that opportunity for me?

6. To what extent will the place I retire to need to provide me with recreational activities (golf, swimming pools, boating, a craft center) or do I want to simply relax/kick back in my retirement location?

7. To what extent are other factors important, such as proximity to a major airport, having a local college nearby, attending VFW or other fraternal organization meetings, ability to board horses or other pets or animals, being a country club member, and so forth.

8. How much money would realistically be needed to adjust my current residence to the one planned for in retirement?

9. How much time would be needed to realistically adjust my current residence to the one planned for in retirement?

10. To what extent do I have to have a back-up plan for changing health conditions and how might those changes impact the retirement residence I'm currently planning? What would I do if those conditions occurred?

[Please return to page 104 to continue reading Chapter 4.]

EXERCISE 2

PRIORITIZING YOUR OPTIONS

You have many choices regarding where to live. Below are some of the alternatives, several of which can be combined into an ideal arrangement.
Identify the top three or four that you would prefer, and make plans accordingly:

_____ My Current Residence

_____ A Warmer Climate

_____ By the Beach

_____ In the Mountains

_____ A Gated Community

_____ A Retirement Community with Many Planned Activities

_____ Smaller "digs", i.e. an Apartment, Townhouse, Co-op

_____ A Rural Setting

_____ A City Setting

_____ A Suburban Lifestyle

_____ A 55+ Community

_____ Living Overseas

_____ A University Town

_____ A Transitional Housing Facility (an independent living to assisted living facility)

_____ Other possible choices—you choose

[Please return to page 105 to continue reading Chapter 4.]

117

EXERCISE 3

EXPLORING RELOCATION

To compare various locations, rate the following factors for each location:
   a) Climate
   b) Recreational, educational, income and civic or religious activities
   c) Social and family relationships
   d) Cost of living
   e) Availability of public and health services
   f) Job possibilities
   g) Availability of public transportation/ airport

Present Housing	A. Importance to you Rate 1-10	B. How well this satisfies this need: Rate 1 - 10	Multiply A x B to determine total for this item.
1. Climate			
2. Recreational, educational, cultural, civic and religious activities			
3. Social and family relationships			
4. Cost of living			
5. Availability of public and health services			
6. Job possibilities			
7. Availability of public transportation			
			Total:

Optional Location #1	A. Importance to you Rate 1-10	B. How well this satisfies this need: Rate 1 - 10	Multiply A x B to determine total for this item.
1. Climate			
2. Recreational, educational, cultural, civic and religious activities			

Optional Location #1	A. Importance to you Rate 1-10	B. How well this satisfies this need: Rate 1 - 10	Multiply A x B to determine total for this item.
3. Social and family relationships			
4. Cost of living			
5. Availability of public and health services			
6. Job possibilities			
7. Availability of public transportation			
			Total:

Optional Location #2	A. Importance to you Rate 1-10	B. How well this satisfies this need: Rate 1 - 10	Multiply A x B to determine total for this item.
1. Climate			
2. Recreational, educational, cultural, civic and religious activities			
3. Social and family relationships			
4. Cost of living			
5. Availability of public and health services			
6. Job possibilities			
7. Availability of public transportation			
			Total:

Compare the 3 possibilities above and determine the strength of each based on your scores. Then prioritize your choices and decide what you might wish to do.

[Please return to page 107 to continue reading Chapter 4.]

EXERCISE 4

COMPARING HOUSING

To compare houses, here are some of the things to consider:
1. Size, convenience, adaptability
2. Privacy, safety, neighborhood
3. Routine maintenance
4. Costs including rent or mortgage, property taxes, insurance
5. Owning or renting
6. Types of housing: condominium, co-op, adult community, life-care residence, time-share, apartment, mobile home, single family house

Take a few moments to rate each of the 3 possible residences below (your current residence and 2 others) according to the factors in the left-hand column. In the first column, you will decide how important that factor is to you on a scale from 1-10 (10 being the highest). In the second column rate how much this factor would be satisfied by the housing choice you are rating. For example, size may be of little importance, perhaps a 4, but your current housing is very well satisfied by size, so you might rate that a 9. Then in the 3rd column, you would multiply these 2 numbers, 4 X 9, and get a total of 36 which you put into the third column. At the end you would add up all the numbers in the third column to come up with your total for that housing choice. Column A numbers would be the same in each of the tables.

Present Housing	A. Importance to you Rate 1-10	B. How well this satisfies this need: Rate 1 - 10	Multiply A x B to determine total for this item.
1. Size			
2. Privacy, safety, neighborhood			
3. Routine maintenance			
4. Costs including rent or mortgage, property taxes, insurance			
5. Owning or renting			
6. Types of housing: condominium, co-op, adult community, life-care residence, time-share, apartment, mobile home, single family house			
			Total:

Optional Location #1	A. Importance to you Rate 1-10	B. How well this satisfies this need: Rate 1 - 10	Multiply A x B to determine total for this item.
1. Size			
2. Privacy, safety, neighborhood			
3. Routine maintenance			
4. Costs including rent or mortgage, property taxes, insurance			
5. Owning or renting			
6. Types of housing: condominium, co-op, adult community, life-care residence, time-share, apartment, mobile home, single family house			
			Total:

Optional Location #2	A. Importance to you Rate 1-10	B. How well this satisfies this need: Rate 1 - 10	Multiply A x B to determine total for this item.
1. Size			
2. Privacy, safety, neighborhood			
3. Routine maintenance			
4. Costs including rent or mortgage, property taxes, insurance			
5. Owning or renting			
6. Types of housing: condominium, co-op, adult community, life-care residence, time-share, apartment, mobile home, single family house			
			Total:

Compare the 3 possibilities above and determine the strength of each based on your score. Then prioritize your choices and decide what you might wish to do.

[Please return to page 108 to continue reading Chapter 4.]

EXERCISE 5

EVALUATING YOUR CURRENT HOUSING

Mark the following "True" or "False" or "I Don't Know":

TOPIC	True	False	I Don't Know
I am happy with my current housing.			
I know where to find resources to help me respond to my questions on housing.			
I am knowledgeable about the many housing choices I have.			
My current community is safe and comfortable for older adults.			
My present home can be adjusted to allow me to live there independently even if my physical condition changes.			
I can afford in-home help if I need it.			
I have considered long-term care insurance to allow me to have in-home care when I need it.			
There is transportation available if I can't drive in later years.			
I am considering investing in two separate dwellings in two different geographic locations— two smaller homes, rather than one larger one as an alternative to moving permanently to another location.			
I have enough equity in my current home to pay for a relocation (including closing costs, moving expenses, taxes, etc.)			
I have considered a reverse mortgage or other financial instruments to pay for future needs.			
I have discussed future housing goals and needs with the important people in my life.			
I have evaluated the impact of changing health on myself and others in considering housing options.			
I can afford to stay in my current house upon retiring and/or when my income is reduced.			

If you answered most of those statements with a "True" response, you are most likely in good control of your housing needs. If you answered "False" or "I Don't Know" on many of these statements, you may have to look into those questions more carefully.

[Please return to page 110 to continue reading Chapter 4.]

SUMMARY OF DECISIONS

PATH 4: BEING AT HOME

Now that you have some background on the topic of housing, "**Being At Home**" and have completed the exercises in this chapter, you should have reached some personal decisions which will later become **key (critical) inputs toward completing your final Action Plan in Chapter 8.** Think about what you would like **to do more of,** or perhaps, what you would like to **do less of** in preparing for your most realistic and fulfilling retirement. Consider in what capacity you see yourself changing your housing goals and actions in the future and why.

☞ What do I want to commit to working on related to my housing in the future:
You Decide

1. I would like to work on determining what the assets, benefits and liabilities are of living where I live now.

2. I would like to work on examining the factors that I should consider in choosing the type of housing I would like to live in now and in the future.

3. I would like to work on determining the factors that will help me to decide whether to relocate or not.

4. I would like to work on discussing my choices and options with the people who are most important to me.

What are these **key decisions?**

Key Decision A

_____

_____

Key Decision B

_____

_____

Key Decision C

_____

_____

Other thoughts, questions, ideas, research that needs to be done, etc.:

Please transfer your decisions into Chapter 8, (Page 232): "Your Action Plan."

CHAPTER 5

PATH 5: VITALIZING RELATIONSHIPS

"Lots of people want to ride with you in the limo, but what you want is someone who will take the bus with you when the limo breaks down."
Oprah Winfrey, TV Show Host, Producer, Actor,
Publisher, Philanthropist (1954----)

In this chapter, you will have the opportunity to:

1. Examine what adjustments you might make to your personal self-identity as you adjust to a new lifestyle in retirement.

2. Determine the distinctions between "Meaningful Relationships" versus "Important Relationships" and apply this knowledge to your relationships.

3. Where appropriate, take stock of your relationships with your spouse/partner, adult children, aging parents, grandchildren, friends, and others. Take a look at what you and they bring and derive from your relationships, and determine the extent changes could/should be made.

4. If you are single, or feel a sense of fear or isolation, review how you might build new relationships outside of the work setting for your future happiness.

Anticipating change

On the day you retire, your world will change. It's more than the loss of your job: your world of work, your daily routine, your sense of structure, and easy contact with your former colleagues will also be gone. To adjust to this transition you will, no doubt, have to adjust your self-identity. In the process you will find that your roles and relationships will also have to be adjusted. In a recent poll conducted by the Investors Group, the largest seller of mutual funds in Canada, (as reported in the Canadian Press by Allan Swift, June 2006) it appears that lots of people over 45 are preparing their finances for retirement, but few feel prepared for the emotional and social aspects of that next stage of their life.

As much as we all more-or-less dream of retirement as a time of relaxation and no one telling us what to do, the reality of retirement can bring on feelings of loss, lower self-esteem, boredom, social isolation and, often, more complicated relationships with spouses/partners who may not have seen so much of us while we were employed.

"Psychological security in retirement is just as important as financial security," says Sara Yogev, a psychologist and author of *For Better or For Worse...But Not for Lunch: Making Marriage Work in Retirement.* Still, so many people fail to prepare and plan for the psychological component.

Consider This
As Elizabeth Holtzman, a counselor in the Faculty and Staff Assistance Program at Amherst College, in Massachusetts, wrote in her article, the *Emotional Aspects of Retirement*, your day is outer-directed when you are employed. It is shaped by the requirements of the job, and success is defined by how well you perform and how well you are compensated. When you retire, your day becomes self-directed. No one is telling you when to get up, when to go to bed. There are no deadlines imposed by a company or job. You are responsible for planning your days and weeks. Success depends on your ability to find happiness in satisfying personal interests and pursuits, human relationships, and creative mental activities.

Holtzman continues: "A critical step in retirement is adjusting to the changes it brings. It means not just accepting and adapting to change, but creating a new lifestyle that is productive and emotionally rewarding."

"Grow old with me! The best is yet to be."
Robert Browning (1812-1889) British poet and playwright

Redefining self-identity

When you work, you learn how to survive within the organization and in many cases change your behavior to do what is required, such as meeting deadlines, completing tasks, and defining success according to organizational requirements. Once you retire, you begin to revert back to your original behavior and to develop a new mind-set.

It is common in our society to allow your work or job title to become a major component of your self-identity. After all, when you first meet someone, the conversation often begins with, "So what do you do?" The day before you retire you can answer that question as you have for many years. The day after, you will need a new answer.

When you start thinking about what work does for you, you can begin to understand why retiring can be unsettling for people. Some of the most important aspects of working, such as having your time structured for you, having challenging assignments, working with people you have gotten to know and enjoy, having a specific role and job description, and being rewarded, both financially and verbally for a job well done are hard to give up. When all of this comes to an end, you can sometimes feel lost; your sense of identity, your self-esteem may falter. When left to your own devices, with a lot of time on your hands, you may become bored, and even worse, depressed. Once the list of chores and repairs that you were waiting to get done "when I retire" are crossed off the list, you may be left with "and now what?" It's the "now what" that this book is attempting to help you plan for.

 All this planning may seem daunting if you were expecting to coast into retirement. Unless you give serious thought now to how you will fill your days, you could be facing an emotional crisis that may feel a lot worse than finding your first job in the labor market.

As your self-identity begins to change, so too will your roles and relationships. While retirement brings the end of your roles as employee and colleague, you will continue to play many other roles as you have throughout your life, such as: child, sibling, friend, cousin, classmate, spouse, colleague, parent, grandparent, and more.

As Marc Freedman, in his book *Prime Time*, commented: "I think the most important thing is we are inventing a whole new stage of life, in between work [the 9-5 routine] and retirement [unstructured leisure time]." It's up to you to determine what will fill this new stage of your life.

 Examine **Exercise 1 (page 139),** "Self-identity: A Conversation with Yourself about Your Relationships with Others in the Coming Years" to explore your own feelings about your relationships in retirement.

As you reviewed your responses to the questions in Exercise 1, did you discover any surprises or information about yourself that you hadn't recognized before? Were there any insights or revelations that had been hidden up to now? Learning more about yourself is always the first step in moving through a transition and managing the change process.

Changing roles, changing relationships

Think about your various roles, and what your relationships are like when you play those roles. For example:

- *Meaningful* relationships bring you joy and energy. These relationships are with people you look forward to having contact with and always feel good about spending time with.
- *Important* relationships may exist because of circumstances, yet not add much to your life. For example, a family member or friend with whom you maintain contact and a cordial relationship for the benefit of others would fit in this category.

 Please complete **Exercise 2 (page 140)**, "Keep on Role-ing" to help you define and redefine your future roles and relationships.

You Decide We all play many roles and parts (as Shakespeare noted) and it is worthwhile to review these and understand that some will be changing as we move into our next phase. What are your changing roles, and are you looking forward to these changes or feeling sad about letting go of former roles or losing them altogether?

"Boomer women are dreaming of retiring to Mars while Boomer men hope to retire to Venus. Boomer men are looking forward to working less, relaxing more, and spending time with their spouse, while boomer women view the dual liberations of empty nesting and retirement as providing new opportunities for career development, community involvement, and continued personal growth."
The New Retirement Survey, 2005, Merrill Lynch

Elizabeth Holtzman also noted in her article: "Making the transition from work to retirement involves sharp and abrupt changes in what is expected of you and what you expect of yourself. Your role as a worker may be over or reduced, but your role as a spouse, partner, parent, or friend doesn't stop, and neither do other multiple roles you play. These roles may change, or in some way be affected by your retirement. People who are unable to let go of the role provided by their work may find it difficult to enjoy their retirement years."

"People change and forget to tell each other."
Lillian Hellman, American playwright (1905-1984)

Your spouse or partner: A frank discussion with your spouse is crucial in making changes go more smoothly. Questions such as where you're going to live, whether you'll be working or volunteering, where you want to travel, and so forth need to be pondered and time to discuss these need to be built into your schedule.

Retirement may create new problems for retirees who are married or in a long-term partnership. Many relationships have been in existence for 20 to 30 years. Patterns have developed about who directs the finances and who takes care of family duties, and retirement may disrupt these familiar roles. Just getting used to being together more regularly may create problems for some couples who do not share common interests. They may find the time together a strain and miss the privacy they previously enjoyed when their partner was working.

Both wives and husbands and partners have ideas, opinions, likes and dislikes; attributes that attracted them to each other which may now be the very things that spark frustration. Whatever the issue, couples need to talk about it in an open and honest way. If you don't like Jim doing the laundry, break the news to him lovingly. If you would like to do the grocery shopping that Natalie has done for years, express your interest and work out an arrangement. A few minutes of heated discussion is better than weeks of repressed anger and resentment.

TIPS

If you are planning to downsize to a smaller house or apartment, it would be valuable to discuss the issue of privacy with your spouse. In a larger dwelling the topic of privacy may not even have entered into your conversation, as you knew where you could retreat to when you wanted to be alone. When square footage is more limited, a discussion regarding where and how you will find your "space" is most important, especially during the winter months when retreating to the outdoors is less attractive. When you were both engaged in more activities outside the home, coming together was much appreciated and even anticipated with pleasure.

Now that you are spending more time at home, and have your private times more interrupted, it is very worthwhile to plan how you will find times and places for your own thoughts and solo activities. Do be sure and include this item on your agenda of discussion topics when considering moving into a smaller house or even if you remain in your current home but are spending more time there.

Consider This

Those who are planning to work part time or engage significantly in volunteer endeavors may not find the issue of downsizing or privacy very important, as you will be out of the house frequently and consistently. In fact, you may find a smaller home to be more convenient as you will have more time for fun and spend less time on maintenance and repairs. Again, choosing your lifestyle and discussing this in detail with your spouse or partner is essential to a satisfying arrangement in the future.

Stop and think about many of the transitions you might have navigated together: marriage, having children, raising your children to adulthood, dealing with a boomerang child, discovering the wonders of being a grandparent, or coping with economic uncertainty. Now think about the happiness all of those times have brought you. Realize that there were some hurts and heartaches along the way, too. You are still together, so you must have done something right. Be proud of your accomplishments! Allow yourself and your spouse/partner time to adjust to this new life phase—just as it took you time to get to where you are today. Remember, you have more than one third of your life ahead of you! Enjoy it!

Rule of Thumb

Rules of Thumb in Relationships: (This can apply to spouses and to just about anyone):

- **Appreciate.** Consider what you most appreciate about the other person. What do you value and respect in that person? What has been satisfying in the past in your relationship? These are the good things. Take the time to appreciate these aspects of your relationship.
- **Plan changes.** Make a list of how you would like things to be with your spouse/partner/significant other. Will things be changing when you retire? What changes can you image taking place? Will these changes be positive or challenging? What do you hope will happen? Will you want to spend more time or less time with your partner? Will your sex life be altered? Delve into your emotional needs and wants and list those out. Encourage your spouse to do the same.
- **What is keeping you back?** Think about the things that have not gone well in the past. Are you holding on to some negative feelings about your significant other? How will those change, increase or diminish when you are spending more time together?
- **Talk it out.** And, most importantly, sit down with your spouse/partner and see if you can make a plan about your relationship to each other in the future. See how creative you can be. Does your partner have the same ideas about the future that you do? Does your significant other want what you want? If not, can you compromise? If your partner wants to continue working and you don't, how will you handle that? If you want to move to a different location and your spouse wants to stay put, how can you compromise and make the most of your differences? Remember the strengths in your relationship; recall the good times together and use those positive aspects to make creative decisions about the future.

As you discuss these topics, remember that this isn't just a one-time conversation. You will need lots of opportunities to chew on these topics. Try not to shy away from these very important discussions; take notes and do research to support your ideas. It's fun to dream about the future. It's even more fun and it can build strength in your relationship when you can turn your dreams into a realistic plan for the future.

 Exercise 3 (Page 142), "Relating to Your Spouse/Partner," may assist you in thinking through your relationship now and how it could conceivably change in retirement.

After completing Exercise 3, and, hopefully, comparing your results with your spouse/partner, you may now have a clearer picture of how the future will be with the most important person in your life. Presumably, you have now identified some initiatives that you both can take to ensure a greater degree of happiness together in the future.

In her article, The *Emotional Aspects of Retirement,* Elizabeth Holtzman, also notes that: "Being single both simplifies and complicates the problems of retirement. It simplifies them because you have only yourself to look after. You can make your own choices. On the other hand, you don't have a partner to share things with or lean on emotionally or financially. Most people have a need to nurture and be nurtured. Being a single retiree may lead to isolation and loneliness, especially if you are a woman."

?
Did You Know?
"Whether widowed, divorced, or single, more and more women are finding a surprisingly practical living arrangement by becoming housemates," according to an article entitled "The New Housemates" by Sarah Mahoney in *AARP the Magazine,* July/August, 2007. Home sharing has become a housing trend for older women. According to the U.S. Census Bureau about 1 percent of women 50 and older currently live with a non-romantic housemate. Besides helping women deal with loneliness, the financial advantages are considerable. As long as there's enough private space and the living arrangements have been well thought through in advance, being a housemate with one or two other women is becoming a more attractive solution to the problem of living alone.

"No road is long with good company."
Turkish proverb

So, how do you get out there and beat the isolation challenge? One approach to redefining relationships is to form new ones. First of all, you need to schedule in activities on your calendar that will help you meet new friends and develop more in-depth relationships with casual friends and family members. You may find that your next-door neighbors are very interesting people and have similar interests.

Revitalizing Your Social Life as a Single Person

Are you thinking about dating? Have you been divorced or widowed? Whatever your situation, you may be considering another serious relationship and want to get started. Sometimes starting a new relationship is frightening and exciting all at the same time. Am I ready for this? If my spouse died, when do I want to start dating? Have I grieved enough? The important thing to consider is whether or not I have accepted that things have changed, I have changed, and I am ready to start a new chapter. This readiness is different for each person and only you will know when it is time to move on.

Do you have some issues that have not been resolved? Do you need outside assistance with these issues? Counseling or coaching may help, especially if you are feeling angry or sad or depressed. These emotional conditions may prevent you from moving ahead in your desires for a new relationship.

Do you want to form a new relationship because others are telling you that you should? Only you know when it is time to begin serious consideration of a new partner in your life. Sometimes it helps to meet someone in a more casual setting—a coffee or lunch would be a good place to start. Or, perhaps, you would like to meet at an event that involves other people. This is also one way to meet someone who has mutual interests.

You Decide

If you feel ready to start meeting people, how do you go about doing that? Again, going to an event that interests you is a good way to meet someone who likes the same activities you do. Another avenue to meeting someone is to tell all your friends and relatives that you are ready to start meeting people. They will be very helpful especially if they know you well. If you choose to use an on-line dating service, which many Boomers are utilizing more and more, do take precautions when actually meeting the person you have only met virtually. Make sure you are in a place with other people and that you have a way to get home.

**You may be only one person in the world
but you may also be the world to one person."**
Anonymous

It may help to list the virtues and characteristics that you would like to find in a serious partner. Then, when you meet someone, this list will be uppermost in your mind. Remember, no one is perfect and neither are you. Flexibility is the key, but be mindful of a person's character as the most important element. Take it slowly and keep your family informed of what you are doing. This way, they can be aware of your whereabouts, as well as help you assess the person you have met. Be sensitive to their opinions, especially if you have children who need to be informed of your activities.

In summary, forming new relationships can be fun as well as a bit scary. But don't be dissuaded just because it's new and full of change. Life is a roller coaster and finding new friends, and perhaps a future partner, can have its ups and downs as well.

FAMILY: Developing closer relationships with family members can be very rewarding. On the other hand, you may find that some family members will assume when you are not "working" that you have nothing to do, and they will request your help for all kinds of reasons.

 If you are not careful, you may find that others are setting your priorities and using your time. You will need to structure your time for yourself, set your own pace, and focus on the contributions you want to make.

Some questions to think about:
- How will retirement affect your relationship with your family, as well as your spouse or partner?
- How will household responsibilities and roles be affected?
- How will you make new friends during retirement?

 As a by-product of your changing circumstances and lifestyle, your relationships with your adult children, aging parents, or grandchildren will most likely be changing. Spending some time with **Exercises 4 through 6 (pages 144-149)** will give you greater insight into what might be. Additionally, these exercises could assist you toward planning actions to achieve greater happiness for yourself as these relationships evolve.

Now that you have completed Exercises 4 through 6, you have most likely realized that your relationships with the people closest to you are changing. Some of these changes may be welcome in your life; others may not. How will you be adjusting to these conditions and how will you take control of your situation?

"A friend may well be reckoned the masterpiece of nature."
Ralph Waldo Emerson, American poet, author (1803-1882)

FRIENDS: Enhancing relationships with current friends or developing new relationships is a task worth undertaking. As we age, friendships become increasingly important and the skill of creating new friendships is also vital. Are you keeping in touch with friends? Do you form friendships outside of the work environment? As our worklife changes, so does our circle of friends. People you once felt close to on a daily basis may not be there if you change jobs or work part time. Will you be keeping close relationships with friends from work, or will these relationships wane when you no longer work with them? How will you keep in touch once work is no longer the place you meet? And, when was the last time you made a new friend?

Research has determined that those who have close relationships with friends are not as prone to anxiety and depression. But, this will take some doing and time commitment. If you make friendship a priority, you may find that the results will be well worth the effort. Keeping in contact on a regular basis with friends, as well as family members, will enable you to maintain and strengthen these relationships.

An interesting endeavor is to make friends with people who are not "just like you." This may mean younger or older folks, people from different occupational backgrounds, people from other parts of your city, people from other cultures and communities. A variety in your friendships is always a tonic for boredom and can

TIPS lead to a more satisfying circle of friends.

Staying in touch can be as easy as e-mail contact or a phone call. A face-to-face meeting at the local coffee shop or a shopping trip together are other ways to communicate and keep the relationship lively.

As we have stated in previous sections, joining an organization in which you have an interest is a wonderful way to make new friends with people who have similar interests. Working as a volunteer is another proven method for meeting new and interesting people. Those who take courses at their local educational institution also have the opportunity to meet new people and create lasting relationships. The final word is that sitting at home and moping about not having friends is not the way to create new friendships.

"Friendship loss is the unexpected fallout of a hurried life. Who has time for friends? They're barely a blip on your screen, until your mother is diagnosed with Alzheimer's and suddenly there's no one to call...Without friends, problems weigh more and pleasures yield less joy."

Marla Paul, author, *The Friendship Crisis, Making, and Keeping Friends When You're Not a Kid Anymore*

As you go through different periods of your life, friendships and other relationships will also go through changes. Be patient with yourself and your friends. We all have our ups and downs. As you continue to stay in touch, you can help others weather their changing situations and in doing so you can strengthen your relationships and build for the future.

And, it's helpful to begin to form friendships with your adult children. You will realize tremendous gains as you let go of the adult/child relationship and develop an adult/adult relationship. You will likely find that your adult children are very interesting people with interests and talents that you may not even have realized.

TIPS

"My father always used to say that when you die, if you've got five real friends, you've had a great life."

Lee Iacocca, American Industrialist (1924---)

If you move away, or your friends move away, it is important to keep in touch. These long distance relationships can seem closer with Internet communication especially with live picture capabilities. The Internet is also a source of friendship where web sites have the capability of matching you with someone who has similar interests.

Making time for friends is the key to all these relationship opportunities. Investing in your friends may be the most profitable investment of your retirement years.

As you look toward the future, you may want to complete **Exercise 7 (page 151)**, "Building on Life's Lessons with Your Partner, Family and Friends." This will give you the opportunity to review the experiences you have had in building relationships in the past and may act as a catalyst to revitalizing current relationships or building new relationships in the coming years.

As you reviewed your relationship successes from the past in Exercise 6, you may now feel more energized to build new relationships and revitalize current ones. While keeping in mind that working on relationships involves change on your part, knowing that you have done this before and that greater happiness awaits at the end of your journey, you may be more motivated to get started.

CHAPTER 5

PATH 5: VITALIZING RELATIONSHIPS

EXERCISES

If you have not already done so, now is your opportunity to complete the following exercises which will assist you in making decisions related to your future relationships with family, friends, and others, thereby, hopefully helping you to consider dealing with alternative situations and opportunities.

Exercise 1   Self-Identity: A Conversation with Yourself about Your Relationships in the Coming Years

Exercise 2: Keep on "Role-ing"

Exercise 3: Relating to Your Spouse/Partner

Exercise 4: Relating to Your Adult Children

Exercise 5: Proactive Grand Parenting

Exercise 6: Relating to Your Aging Parents

Exercise 7: Building on Life's Lessons with Your Partner, Family and Friends

At the conclusion of the exercises is a **"Summary of Decisions"** page, which will allow you to think through some of the thoughts and ideas you have been gathering in completing this chapter. Please take some time to evaluate the information you have both reviewed and created, and then summarize some key points in writing that you would like to pursue in putting together your final action plan in this book's last chapter, **"Your Action Plan...Putting It All Together."**

EXERCISE 1

SELF-IDENTITY: A CONVERSATION WITH YOURSELF ABOUT YOUR RELATIONSHIPS IN THE COMING YEARS

What do you look forward to most about retirement?

What concerns do you have about transitioning from work to leisure?

What will you do with your free time?

Think about people you know who have retired. Do you want the same kind of retirement experience? What do you want to do differently?

Do you believe your personal value stems from your job?
- If so, to what extent do you think you will see yourself lacking in value once you no longer have a job?
  Not at all _____ A little _____ A lot _____
- To what extent will you worry about how others will perceive you?
  Not at all _____ A little _____ A lot _____
- How do you plan to deal with this, if it's an issue?

[Please return to page 127 to continue reading Chapter 5.]

EXERCISE 2

KEEP ON "ROLE-ING"

Review below the list of roles that you play with others and add any additional ones from your own experience.

In the columns below:

1) Record the role you play and name of the person with whom you are having that relationship.

2) Check the column(s) M (*meaningful*) and/or I (*important*) that describe the relationship you have with that person.

3) Indicate the amount of time you spend on that relationship each month.

4) Record your comments reflecting what you want to change, modify or improve in that relationship in the coming years.

5) Answer the questions that follow the chart.

Possible Roles that you play:

Spouse/Significant Other	Parent/Step-parent	Grandparent
Son/Daughter/in-law	Niece/Nephew	Aunt/Uncle
Cousin	Sister/Brother	Friend(s)
Religious org. member	Supervisor	Work Colleague
Boss/Subordinate	Classmate/Alumni	Member
Community volunteer	Fund raiser	Lover
Professional Assn Member	Club member	Neighbor

My Role/Name of person with whom I am having this relationship	M	I	Time/month	Comments: What changes do I want to effect in the coming years with this person?
Examples: Spouse/ My spouse Fran	X	X	150 hr	Create romantic getaway every other month
Parent/ My daughter Josephine	?	X	5 hr	Call twice a week on the telephone
				(Continue on next page)

My Role/Name of person with whom I am having this relationship	M	I	Time/month	Comments: What changes do I want to effect in the coming years with this person?

Do you see anything that surprises you?

Which of your existing roles will change?

Do you like the way it appears you will be spending your time?

Do you think you will have trouble letting go of the role(s) provided by work? If so, how will that affect your retirement years?

How do you expect your role and relationship with your spouse/partner to be affected?

What are your concerns about the expected changes? What do you think your spouse's/partner's concerns are?

[Please return to page 128 to continue reading Chapter 5.]

EXERCISE 3

RELATING TO YOUR SPOUSE/PARTNER

It is imperative that you and your spouse/partner share to a large extent the same values and vision of your future. This exercise is intended to see the extent to which you are both emotionally and financially ready to share the future together. It is advisable for you and your spouse/partner to do this exercise separately and then talk over your results. Obviously, there will be differences in your answers, as all relationships have differing opinions and desires. The trick is to discuss these openly and determine suitable compromises that allow both individuals to enjoy their future both separately and together.

1. On the range indicated below, put an X on how you would describe the quality of the current relationship between you and your spouse/partner:

We are quite close   It is not good

_____

2. On the range indicated below, put an X on how you would describe how well you each respect each other's privacy, possessions, visitors, circumstances:

Highly respectful of each   Little respect
others' freedom of action   for the other's
and don't intercede   decision-making
                                                   + criticism &
                                                   retribution

_____

3. On the range indicated below, put an X indicating the extent you can strengthen or desire to proactively change your relationship with each other:

Easily changed or   Extremely
improved   difficult to change

_____

4. To what extent are there financial or economic issues troubling your relationship? Is this based on unequal earning power or previous savings? If so, what are the implications for retirement? Could your spouse/partner support you in your retirement? Does this create friction? Do you anticipate future dependency and what are the implications for your relationship?

5. What specific activities do you and your spouse/partner enjoy together and separately? Do you anticipate changes in the future? Do you desire to increase or decrease the activities you do together or separately and what are the implications?

6. Are there financial or emotional issues regarding your children? Is this affecting your relationship with your spouse/partner? Do you need support from your children and, if so, has this been discussed? With what results?

7. Have you discussed with your children the possibility that they may have to be care givers to you and/or your spouse in the future? How do your adult children feel about care giving? To what extent have you discussed this with them and your spouse/partner or is this in need of discussion?

8. How do you feel about care giving? Are you resentful, or pleased that it can be done? Do you see this changing? Do you need for others to participate in providing assistance? When can a change be initiated?

9. Identify your thoughts on anticipating future changing circumstances with your spouse/partner. Examples: Your relocation, a job loss, a serious illness, etc. How would such circumstances affect your retirement plans and your relationship?

> Note: Don't forget to schedule in the fun times together on your calendar. They are essential to a quality and well-balanced relationship.

[Please return to page 131 to continue reading Chapter 5.]

EXERCISE 4

RELATING TO YOUR ADULT CHILDREN

Some retirees have to support their adult children (and their families), while other retirees choose to do so. Regardless of the reason, it is important to assess the impact of doing so —both financially and emotionally.

1. On the range indicated below, put an X on how you would describe the quality of the current relationship between you and each of your adult children:

We are quite close   It is not good

_____

2. On the range indicated below, put an X on how you would describe how well you each respect each other's privacy, possessions, visitors, circumstances:

Highly respectful of each   Little respect
others' freedom of action   for the other's
and don't intercede   decision-making
                                                               + criticism and
                                                               retribution

_____

3. On the range indicated below, put an X indicating the extent you can strengthen or proactively change your relationship with each of your children:

Easily changed or   Extremely
improved   difficult to change

_____

4. To what extent are your adult children capable of supporting themselves? Conversely, could they support you in your retirement? Is there any current or future anticipated dependency? What needs to be put in place to reduce dependency?

5. What specific activities do you perform for your adult child(ren)?   How often? What does this cost in dollars? How much in time? List the dollar expenditures:

What is paid for? How much? How often?

Conversely, do you need support from your children and if so has this been discussed? With what results?

6. How do your adult children feel about care giving? To what extent have you discussed this with them or is this in need of discussion?

7. How do you feel about care giving?   Are you resentful, or pleased that it can be done? Do you see this changing? Do you need for others to participate in providing assistance? When can a change be initiated?

8. Identify your thoughts on anticipating future changing circumstances with respect to each adult child and their families. Examples: Their relocation, a job loss, a serious illness, etc. How would such circumstances affect your retirement plans and your relationship?

[Please return to page 133 to continue reading Chapter 5.]

EXERCISE 5

PROACTIVE GRAND-PARENTING

Grand-parenting is a wonderful opportunity to give to others and also to get much in return.

Listed below are opportunities for you and for your grandchildren (and adult children). Rate each item as to the most potential benefit to grandchildren and separately rate what gives you the greatest potential reward.

4 = Great benefit   3 = Beneficial
2 = Not very beneficial   1 = Not important/not relevant

Item:	Benefit to Grand Child(ren)	Benefit to Me Personally
Spending as much time as possible with my grandchild(ren) who live close to me, i.e. they are my immediate family		
Being the primary adult raising my grandchild(ren)		
Freeing up my adult children's time by babysitting for my grandchild(ren), when needed		
Going on vacation with grandchildren		
Having my grandchild(ren) visit with me at my home because I am in a different location than where they live		
Occasionally visiting with grandchild(ren), playing with them, telling them stories, or developing a unique relationship with them		
Buying gifts for my grandchild(ren)		
Giving or leaving money for my grandchild(ren)'s college education		

As you think about these ratings, try to imagine what changes you would like to make in your relationships with your grandchild(ren) and use the chart on the next page to record your thoughts.

There is also a second chart provided on page 148 to help you more carefully evaluate the quality of your relationship with each of your grandchildren.

Establishing Priorities

Based on the ratings you identified on the previous page, use the following chart to determine <u>what actions</u> could you take to strengthen your relationship with your grandchild(ren) or to better provide for their upbringing? What would you derive from this?

Begin Doing or Increase Doing NOW:	Benefit to My Grand Child(ren):	Benefit to Me:
Begin Doing _____ (At A Future Date):	Benefit to My Grand Child(ren):	Benefit to Me:

Relationship(s) to grandchildren

Think about and describe the quality of the relationship you have with each grandchild. What do you and each grandchild derive from the relationship? Regardless of how good it is, how can it be further improved? Use the chart below to further clarify and plan your actions:

Grandchild: _____ Current age: _____	Quality of Our Relationship	How to Further Improve It?
Grandchild: _____ Current age: _____		
Grandchild: _____ Current age: _____		
Grandchild: _____ Current age: _____		

[Please return to page 133 to continue reading Chapter 5.]

EXERCISE 6

RELATING TO YOUR AGING PARENTS

This exercise provides you with a serious inquiry into the current and future needs of your parent(s) and helps identify ways to promote future well-being for you and your parent(s).

1. How would you describe the physical, mental, and psychological conditions (and well-being) of your parent(s)?

2. How would you describe your relationship to your parent(s)?
    * What would strengthen it?
    * What barriers exist that prevent this from strengthening?
    * What has been tried?
    * What needs to be tried?
    * How do you foresee your future relationship?

3. If you could do so, what would you like to know (learn) from your parent(s)? What questions would you ask? Would there be a particularly good time to investigate or learn new facts?

4. How prepared are you to deal with the physical deterioration of your parent(s)? What needs to be done now or in the near future to deal with these future events?

5. What is your parent(s) attitude toward their care givers? Can or should this be changed?

6. What is the cost of parental care giving? Where are the funds coming from and how much is left for future assistance? To what extent will you need to contribute to future care giving? How much?

7. Do you know your parent(s) final life plans, arrangements, and resting place?

8. Does a "Power of Attorney" exist for care of your parent(s)? Do you know the location of wills and other personal effects belonging to your parent(s)? Is there an executor for their will? Who is it?

9. Is there more you can do to understand your parent('s') current needs? What questions would you like to ask to learn more? What steps need to be taken to improve your knowledge or to better fulfill your personal knowledge in this regard?

10. Who else (e.g. siblings, other relatives, attorney, funeral home) do you need to consult with to plan for future action/events?

[Please return to page 133 to continue reading Chapter 5.]

EXERCISE 7

BUILDING ON MY LIFE'S LESSONS: WITH MY PARTNER, FAMILY AND FRIENDS

In reflecting upon life, many individuals dwell on "What might have been," or decisions they wish they had not made, or unplanned circumstances that occurred causing them considerable unhappiness. It is easy to get into a "negative" mind game.

It is far better to concentrate on one's successes in life, i.e. times that brought you happiness, pride, a sense of accomplishment, recognition, and so forth. It is said that success in life is partially luck and circumstance, but more important is the ability to create circumstances, develop skills and knowledge as well as the attitude that fosters successful relationships.

Building on My Relationship Experience

This is an opportunity for me to examine or reflect on the successes in my life and then apply them to my future, particularly to my future in retirement.

What was "My Greatest Relationship Lesson or Success?"

What was "My 2nd Most Important Relationship Lesson or Success?"

What did I do to create this lesson?

If I had my dream, what would my single greatest future relationship success be? How would it feel? Who would share this happiness with me?

What should or could I do to create this future success? When will I start to create this future success?

[Please return to page 135 to continue reading Chapter 5.]

SUMMARY OF DECISIONS

PATH 5: VITALIZING RELATIONSHIPS

Now that you have some background on the topic of "**Vitalizing Relationships**" and have completed the exercises in this chapter, you should have reached some personal decisions which will later become **key (critical) inputs toward completing your final Action Plan in Chapter 8.** Think about what you would like **to do more of,** or perhaps, what you would like to **do less of** in preparing for your most realistic and fulfilling retirement. Consider in what capacity you see yourself changing your relationships in the future and why.

You
Decide

What do I want to commit to working on related to Vitalizing Relationships?

1. I would like to work on adjusting my personal self-identity.

2. I would like to work on determining which the most important relationships in my life, are and how I would like to enhance or improve them.

3. I would like to work on taking stock of my relationships with a partner/spouse, adult children, aging parents, grandchildren, friends and others and determine whether I want to enhance or change any of those relationships.

4. If I am feeling a sense of fear or isolation, I would like to work on developing new relationships and determining how I might go about doing that.

What are your **key decisions?**

Key Decision A

_____

_____

Key Decision B

_____

_____

Key Decision C

_____

_____

Other thoughts, questions, ideas, research that needs to be done, etc.:

Please transfer your decisions into Chapter 8 (Page 234): "Your Action Plan."

CHAPTER 6

PATH 6: WORK IS NO LONGER WORK

"Doing what you love is the cornerstone of having abundance in your life."
Wayne Dyer, American self-help advocate, author and lecturer (1940---)

In this chapter, you will have the opportunity to:
1. Discover the latest trends related to working in retirement.
2. Learn about people in their 60's, 70's and even 80's who are still working.
3. Learn how to balance work and other pursuits to achieve the ideal retirement for you.
4. Learn how to manage the changes that will occur when we shift from the usual 9-5 routine to the next stage of our lives.

For some of us, the idea of not working is anticipated with joy and for others with dread. Most of us can weigh the pros and cons as well as factor in other realities – financial, health, family, our skills, etc. Each of us knows some limitations to our choices. Some have already reached conclusions about whether to continue working, what that work will look like, and how to balance work and other pursuits. Others want to formulate new plans and discover or fulfill new opportunities.

Working in retirement sounds like an oxymoron. But, what we are finding is that more people in their 50's, 60's and 70's who think of themselves as retired, are definitely not. This is the time when people are finding ways to follow their dreams, be engaged in work that they have always wanted to do and answer a calling that wasn't available to them when they were in the earlier stages of their careers.

Consider This

For most, the word retirement is part of a major change. For many, it means that you will no longer spend more hours in an organization than you spend with your family or friends. So much of our energy, self-image, time and focus are based in our jobs that leaving the world of work behind can be both joyful and frightening. For some, continuing to work will definitely be an option; for others, a "must have" reality.

The exercises in this chapter provide a way to think through one's options. Even though you may or may not realize it, you are the repository of talents, skills and qualities that you have developed over the years; and it is these same qualities that may guide you into finding work that you love. And even if you have already made some decisions, these exercises will help ensure that you have not overlooked any important factors that may impact your choices.

"A bit of advice given to a young Native American at the time of his initiation: 'As you go the way of life, you will see a great chasm. Jump. It is not as wide as you think.'"

Once a person reaches 65, it is estimated that the average life expectancy for men will be 80 and the average for women is 84. So for most people 25 years or more of retirement is a strong probability. Work – part time, full time, starting a business, or consulting, in one's present field or a new one – are all options more people are considering.

Joseph Campbell, American professor, writer and orator (1904-1987)

When thinking about what you would like to do, consider an apprenticeship or an internship in a career that appeals to you. Many professionals can use an assistant and, while you shadow your "mentor," you will also learn about how it feels to work in that environment. You might desire to start your own business or do free-lancing. And so, it would be wise to talk to someone who made a similar and successful career change and learn from their experience.

Did You Know?

According to a study released in December 2005 by the Families and Work Institute and Boston College's Center on Aging and Work, older workers who are self-employed are likelier to be happier with their work situation than those who work for someone else. That doesn't mean that they work less; in fact they work

154

longer hours than the wage-and-salary workers; this simply means that they have more control over their work, more autonomy, more flexibility and they earned more, as related by Ellen Galinsky, President of the Families and Work Institute, a non-profit group in New York.

For many Boomers, a retirement job will be the perfect time to begin a second career. According to a recent survey titled the "2006 Merrill Lynch New Retirement Study," the top ten retirement jobs that Boomers look forward to having are:

- Consultant (27%)
- Teacher or Professor (20%)
- Customer Greeter (15%)
- Tour Guide (13%)
- Retail Sales Clerk (13%)
- Bookkeeper or Auditing Clerk (10%)
- Home Handyman (10%)
- Bed and Breakfast Owner or Manager (9%)
- Security Screener (8%)
- Real Estate Agent (7%)

"I enjoy my work so much that I have to be pulled away from my work into leisure."
Ralph Nader, American attorney, Presidential candidate and political activist (1934---)

You
Decide

Retirees work for a variety of reasons. Which ones apply to your situation?

- Current income is not sufficient to maintain my desired quality of life.
- I need intellectual stimulation and challenge.
- I don't have medical benefits.
- I need a reason to get up in the morning and stay active.
- Life doesn't seem to have a purpose anymore.
- I don't feel useful; I used to like helping people.
- Work used to be fun; I enjoyed it and don't have anything to replace it.
- All my friends were at work and I don't have new friends to replace them.
- I like to learn new things.
- I can't seem to find new goals and pursue a vision.

As this list indicates, most retirees have more than one reason to consider working! For some, the choice to work is driven by finances, or a need for medical benefits. Others have planned a second career. Some will be asked to delay retirement as organizations begin to

155

feel the impact of the "Boomer Brain Drain." For some, the choice is psychological: a need to ease into retirement, not feel that one is just jumping off a cliff into a rocking chair! Moving from long hours at a job to freedom to do as one chooses is a change that calls for planning.

The range of choices available is extensive:
- part time
- full time
- flexible
- consulting
- starting your own business
- staying in your present position
- moving into an entirely different field
- working part of the year in one state and part in another
- working for a non-profit as a board member or as a volunteer.

And everything points to the choices becoming a longer list as companies realize the brain drain that is occurring as Boomers leave their organizations.

According to the *Pittsburgh Business Times*, June 1, 2007, companies are finding that rehiring retirees creates more experienced staff. Attracting retirees back to the work force is one way companies are dealing with lack of talent in their industry. And with more and more people entering into the retirement years, this talent pool is continuing to grow. Employers are beginning to realize that retirees are experienced, whether working part-time or full-time and they bring knowledge and skills that can also help train the next generation. What attracts retirees back to a former employer or to a new employer is flexible hours or job sharing. There are also several benefit programs that will help to attract retired workers; these include: employee assistance and work-life programs, elder care assistance, retirement and financial planning, adaptive and assistive technology, ergonomic adjustments, health care coverage for less than full-time employment and opportunities to mentor younger employees. If losing pension benefits is a concern, companies are taking back former employees as subcontractors or through an employment or temporary agency. Companies are finally waking up to the fact that hiring older workers is a good business strategy.

It should come as no surprise that most individuals planning retirement still plan to work in retirement. This is clearly a significant economic, philosophical, psychological, and cultural realignment of what is meant by retirement. So what have pollsters found these days?

- Just about half of working Americans say they expect to have enough money to live comfortably in retirement, down about 10% in just 5 years. No wonder that over half of Americans are "very" or "moderately" worried about financing their retirement. Perhaps this is why well over half of these working Americans indicate a strong interest in working either part-time or intermittently in retirement. Additionally, retirement is also being pushed back by many who had previously planned to retire earlier; now about a third of workers plan to retire only after age 65 compared to about 10% who planned to work that long in the mid-1990's.
- About a third of working adults are somewhat concerned or fear "losing a sense of purpose" in their lives when retired. Again, perhaps this is why a recent Gallup study found: 71% with post-graduate education, 64% with college, and 60% of those with no college education indicate they will likely work in retirement.

Making an informed decision about whether to work beyond retirement will help make yours a happier and more fulfilling retirement. Many of the things you'll learn in the following exercises will also be of value in planning leisure and volunteer activities. (For more on Volunteer activities, please consult the chapter: "Time to Do Good…and For Good Times.")

You Decide   The following questions ask for some introspection on your part and are intended to help you think through your own views of work, what options and opportunities exist and how work fits into retirement.

Self-Assessment

Questions	Notes to Myself
1. Do I need to work in retirement for the money or for health benefits?	
2. If not for money, do I want to find new work to keep active, to meet people, to fulfill a dream pursuit, or for some other reason?	
3. If it's for financial reasons, is it to replace a position I had filled so as to supplement my income, or to continue building wealth?	
4. How much work do I want: to work part-time, full time, seasonally, on-call, or on a project basis?	
5. How long do I plan to continue working…for a short time, until my spouse/partner retires, for several years until pensions or social security kick in, for many years following onset of "retirement", or until what age?	
6. How far am I prepared to travel and how many hours per week would I plan to work, including commuting time?	

Questions	Notes to Myself
7. Where would I like to work: with others at a corporation with the politics it may entail, at my home office with few disturbances, in a retail store with all their rules about working on holidays, or elsewhere?	
8. With whom do I want to work: alone, with my spouse or partner, with my prior coworkers or colleagues, with my children or family members, for a voluntary/non-profit organization for the elderly, ill or needy?	
9. What current interests/passion/unfilled dream do I have that could lead into a new career?	
10. What competencies or special skills would I like to use or learn to use in a new work role?	
11. Is there a hobby or interest that I could blend or convert into a business or money maker?	
12. Do I have interests in any of the following: crafts, cars, photography, flowers, music, art, food, electronics, pets, the stock market and investing, etc?	
13. What have I learned from my previous job experiences that I would like to repeat or emulate in a future work endeavor? Why?	
14. What have I learned from my previous job experiences that I want to avoid in a future work endeavor? Why?	
15. Am I willing to get further education or serve an internship if my job in retirement requires it?	
16. Will working in retirement give me the proper family life-balance that I would be seeking (i.e. time to take vacation trips, for hobbies, to attend sporting and other events, time to visit with family and friends, etc.)?	
17. Is there any person, event, or something I strongly value in my life that could affect my choice of work decision?	
18. To what extent could future health, family, or other important considerations affect my decision to work?	
19. Whom should I speak to for advice or counsel before I make my future choices about working in retirement?	
20. What if I did not work?	

Many of the questions here will be explored in greater depth as you continue with this section on work. If you have made a decision not to seek employment once you retire, the exercises may still be helpful to you in making other choices based on what you value, enjoy, do well, want to learn or hope to avoid in retirement.

Please turn to **Exercise 1 (page 167)**, "Working Full-time or Part-time" and **Exercise 2 (page 168)**, "Working for Money or For Other Personal Needs" to gain a greater sense of your thoughts on future employment. Review these questions about your need to work in retirement and what you would like to do.

Assuming you completed Exercise 1 and 2, did you formulate any thoughts about what kind of work you would like to be doing in retirement, and how much money you would need to earn?

Another way to think about the work that you might choose to do in retirement is to imagine that someone is asking you the following questions. As you take the time to think of the answers, think about how you are feeling as you respond to these questions. Try to supply as much detail as you can when you answer the questions. Think about what your family and the society you were raised in thought about work. Think of how work was valued, and which jobs were respected when you were growing up. How were you influenced by these values?

The hardest question might be this one: How has your life been affected by what you learned from your family and your culture?

When you changed jobs, or lost a job, how did you feel? Were you relieved not to have to work and to be able to collect unemployment? Were you unsure of what you would do each day if you didn't have a job to show up for?

 You Decide Ask yourself the following questions and allow yourself to spend time thinking about your answers. The following questions ask for some introspection on your part; they are intended to help you think through your own views of work, what options and opportunities exist and how work fits into retirement.

Clearly, there is no right or wrong answer to any of these questions. The point of this exercise is to help you see what part work has played in your life, what you learned about the value or necessity of work growing up, and what you have enjoyed, or hated, about work.

The questions are to help you to analyze how you view work and whether you want to include some aspect of working in your retirement years.

1. Think back and describe your favorite jobs.
2. What were your least favorite jobs?
3. What job or jobs stand out in your memory of your entire work history?
4. Did you change jobs, or want to change jobs at any age while working? Please explain.
5. If you are working, why do you work now?

159

6. If you would prefer not to be working now, please explain.
7. What does work mean to you? Is it a necessity, an obligation, a joy, a part of each or something else?
8. What did you learn about work from your family, your culture, the people around you, and their values about work?
9. Do you have any particular memories about a friend or relative who had a job you thought was special, or exciting?
10. If you are currently working, how long have you worked where you work now? Do you have plans to change jobs, or wish you could? Why?
11. Do you work because you have to or because you want to? Please explain.
12. If you could have an ideal job, what would it be? Why is this your ideal job?
13. Would you like to retire, or have you tried retirement?
14. If you could retire, what would you visualize your ideal retirement to be?
15. Do you volunteer, or would you like to volunteer? If so, what would you like to do as a volunteer?

Having taken time to think about the answers to these questions, what have you discovered about yourself? Look at the pattern of your answers. Do you fit into the pattern of needing to work for structure, or for fun? Have you enjoyed work in the past and are now looking for something new to do? Are you afraid not to work? Do you dread the boredom that may ensue if you are not working?

Now that you have examined more thoroughly your need to work and your motivations underlying your need to work and have decided that working will be a part of your retirement plan, it is time to consider how you can find the job that you desire.

The Internet

An afternoon on the Internet will reveal a number of companies that recognize the value of older workers and that are finding ways to enlist their services. Volunteer organizations such as the "Executive Services Corps" find ways to use your expertise to help non-profit organizations. Services like "Grey Hair Management" help retirees find projects or positions. All of these sources can identify possible opportunities for employment, volunteer work, consulting, or some combination of these.

The result of all these possibilities is that you may find answers to questions such as: "How will I spend my time? "How will I make sure I have health insurance or enough income to last throughout my lifetime?" "How can I make a difference to others?" etc.

"Your imagination is your preview of life's coming attractions."
Albert Einstein, Theoretical Physicist (1879-1955)

 What would your job in retirement look like? How would it be different from the job you have now or recently left? Each of us can think of some things that are important to us about any job, and **Exercise 3 (page 172),** the "Satisfiers and Dissatisfiers Exercise," may help you to become clearer about what you would like to see or avoid in a job in retirement. Take a few minutes to look it over and complete it.

What did you learn in Exercise 3 that further refines your possible plans for performing work in the early retirement phase of your life?

 Now that you have had an opportunity to reflect on what appeals to you about possible job opportunities, as well as what you would rather not spend time doing at work in the future, the next step is to think about where you would like to work? **Exercise 4 (page 175),** "The Work Environment Exercise" may help you get greater clarity about where you could perform the work that you prefer doing. This exercise may help you discover where your interests lie.

If you completed Exercise 4, what did you discover about the work environment that you favor? Can you find or create work that would meet your desires?

And speaking of desires, remember that in the introductory chapter, "Envision Your Ideal Retirement", you were asked to examine the values most important to you. Quickly look at **Exercise 5 (page 177),** "My Values," toward the end of this chapter and read the instructions. Also refer to the work you did in the introductory chapter. You may find reaffirmation of your earlier thoughts. If not, were there discoveries that could set you on a new course of planning in retirement? What values came to the foreground that will impact your decision-making related to working or volunteering during your retirement years?

"The people who get on in this world are the people who get up and look for the circumstances they want, and, if they can't find them, make them."
George Bernard Shaw, Irish dramatist, literary critic and socialist (1856-1955)

 By now, most of us have already made some decisions about what work we would like to do in retirement based on past experiences in the working world. Let's see if this is true for you. **Exercise 6 (page 178),** "Life's Lessons: Work-Life Successes and Set-backs" can teach us a lot about what we can learn from our past. Please consider taking a few minutes to revisit what past successes or perhaps setbacks could be instructive in dealing with future work arrangements.

Now that you completed Exercise 6, have you discovered any lessons out of the past that could affect your planning a future which will be both challenging and pleasing?

"Life can only be understood backwards, but it must be lived forward."
Soren Kierkegaard, Danish philosopher and writer (1813-1855)

You Decide — Finally, no examination of how you might pursue work activities in the future would be complete without thinking through the other half of the job equation – you! What skills, knowledge and experience do you bring to an employer or project? When asked what you have achieved in your career, what would you list as accomplishments? If you thought about jobs you have had throughout your working life, would you spot patterns to help you define what you do well, or would rather not do? Would you realize that over time there are activities that you have enjoyed being involved in whenever you had the chance? The unique thing about retirement is that reviewing some of those characteristics can sometimes help us to think of different choices and consider options that we have been overlooking.

The world of work is changing rapidly – each of us needs to understand what skills we bring to everything we do, because this is what we have to offer an employer, or what we will use in setting up our own businesses or as volunteers.

"You have to deal with the fact that your life is your life."
Alex Haley, American writer (1921-1992)

Please turn to **Exercise 7 (page 180)**, "Career Competencies" and complete the assessment. Use the Career Competencies Exercise to consider what you bring to the things you do. This is an exercise that gives you a way of thinking through what strengths you bring to everything you do. Competencies are behaviors that people engage in, no matter what they are doing. A behavior combined with experience results in a personal strength or skill. The value of the listed competencies is not dependent upon whether you are working as a volunteer, in a corporate or retail setting, or in an industrial or construction site.

Exercise 8 (page 184), "Strengths and Weaknesses" will give you the opportunity to summarize your strengths and weaknesses and allow you to acknowledge these with an eye to determining where you want to utilize your strengths in the world of work.

162

Now that you have completed Exercises 7 and 8, what conclusions can you draw from these exercises? Are you now more clear on where you want to spend your working time and what activities would be most fulfilling for you? Do take the time to acknowledge yourself for all the skills and talents that you have accumulated over the years. These are your strengths and form the backbone of your future decisions regarding working.

"The person who has lived the most is not the one with the most years but the one with the richest experiences."
Jean Jacques Rousseau, Swiss political philosopher and essayist (1712-1778)

Is work "The Means" or "The End Result" that we are after? Is it the challenge (the process) or the result that we are after? Is it intended to prove something to ourselves or to others? And…where does the development of new relationships, filling one's time, making money, leaving a legacy, helping others, helping ourselves, finding escapism, learning something new, or finding structure in our lives…among other outcomes and arrangements… fit into our lives, especially in the years of retirement? This chapter and its embedded exercises exist to answer many of these questions for you.

CHAPTER 6

PATH 6: WORK IS NO LONGER WORK

EXERCISES

If you have not already done so, now is your opportunity to complete the following exercises, which will assist you in making decisions related to working or not working, thereby, hopefully, helping you to consider dealing with alternative solutions and opportunities.

Exercise 1: Working Full-time or Part-time

Exercise 2: Working for Money or for Other Personal Needs

Exercise 3: Satisfiers and Dissatisfiers

Exercise 4: Work Environment

Exercise 5: Your Values

Exercise 6: Life's Lessons: Work-Life Successes and Set-backs

Exercise 7: Career Competencies

Exercise 8: Strengths and Weaknesses

At the conclusion of the exercises is a "**Summary of Decisions**" page, which will allow you to think through some of the thoughts and ideas you have been gathering in completing this chapter. Please take some time to evaluate the information you have both reviewed and created, and then summarize some key points in writing that you would like to pursue in putting together your final action plan in this book's last chapter, "**Your Action Plan...Putting It All Together.**"

EXERCISE 1

WORKING FULL-TIME OR PART-TIME

Questions:

1. How many dollars are you missing to live the lifestyle you will require in retirement? None or $ _____ per month?

2. If you want or need to work, how many hours per week would it be? _____/week.

3. What work would you be doing in retirement?

Likely position #1:

Working for whom? _____
Alternative position #2:

Working for whom? _____
Alternative position #3:

Working for whom? _____

4. To what extent is it possible to accomplish finding or doing the jobs listed above? Would you need to network and get contacts? When would you begin the process of planning for your work transition (assuming that you would discontinue working in your present capacity)?

5. Besides financial remuneration, what would you hope to gain from working? List these other benefits:

6. For how long would you plan to work? Under what circumstances would you stop working?

7. With whom and when would you plan to review these plans?

[Please return to page 159 to continue reading Chapter 6.]

EXERCISE 2

WORKING FOR MONEY OR
OTHER PERSONAL NEEDS

Item	Strongly Agree	Agree	Neither Agree or Disagree	Disagree	Strongly Disagree
1. I must work in retirement to "make ends meet", i.e. I will have insufficient money to maintain my current lifestyle.					
2. I will need to work for the insurance coverage.					
3. Working will help me feel fulfilled.					
4. I will need to work to "get out of the house."					
5. I will want "pocket change", that "psychological cushion" to easily afford the things I will want to do or have.					
6. Work is not for the money; work will provide the means to help others in need (my children, community, etc.)					
7. I will work to keep busy, to avoid boredom.					

168

Item	Strongly Agree	Agree	Neither Agree or Disagree	Disagree	Strongly Disagree
8. Work is a way to meet other people.					
9. Work is needed as a means to fulfill my identity.					
10. Work is like a hobby to me…I enjoy it.					

If you rated an item "Strongly Agree" or "Agree," this would signify that you attach value to a particular category. These categories are:

A. Need for financial remuneration   Typically #1, #2, and #5 above

B. Need for status (and perhaps power or control) Typically #3 and #9

C. Need for a sense of value/accomplishment   Typically #6, #9 and #10

D. Need to occupy my time   Typically #4 and #7

E. Need for socialization   Typically #4 and #8

Assuming the values above are correct, how do you look at work meeting your needs?

A. For those seeking <u>Financial Remuneration</u> from work in retirement:
1. How much money do you need to earn?
2. Precisely how short are you of your targeted financial needs?
3. How do you plan to earn the monies needed?
4. How long precisely will you need to work?
5. Can you project how successful you will be in obtaining work to fulfill your needs?
6. What work will you do?
7. Who will hire you or use the products or services you bring to market?
8. Are you now capable of developing a plan to keep working well into your retirement years?
9. What do you need to do <u>now</u> to ensure you have marketability to work in your retirement?
10. If you continue working, can you think of it or call it retirement?

11. Is there a way to gain the monetary returns you derive from work without working? If you could secure money elsewhere, how could this be done, and when would you want to do this?

12. What are the consequences of not working? To what extent can you live with less money?

B. For those seeking <u>Status (and perhaps Power and Control)</u> from work in retirement:
1. Why is your identity wrapped up in what you do?
2. Or to what extent is work defining who you are?
3. What is the monetary or psychological value of work? Does status lie in your mind or those of others? Who counts? Why?
4. How easily can status be changed and what would occur if it changed?
5. If status includes power or control, for whose benefit does it exist? How would loss of power or control affect your life? What are the consequences? Can you derive complete satisfaction in life without the status that you derive from work? If so, how could this be done, and when would you want to do this?

C. For those seeking <u>a Sense of Value/Accomplishment</u> from work in retirement?
1. What value does your work bring to others? Specifically to whom?
2. What actual and psychological value does your work offer you...what are the benefits?
3. Will you continue seeing as an appropriate "return on your investment" for the time spent working...for you and others? For how long? Will it diminish over time?
4. Can you derive complete satisfaction in life in retirement without the sense of accomplishment that you derive from work? Is there a way to substitute other activities for work to derive the same sense of satisfaction? What would those activities be? If substitutes exist, how could this be done, and when would you want to do this?

D. For those seeking <u>to occupy their time</u> by working in retirement:
1. What is it about work that makes you feel that you are using it to spend time usefully?
2. Are you committed to working to help "pass the day", use it to change the daily routine, or is it to avoid dealing with other issues (for example, family relationships).
3. If you did not have to work to keep yourself occupied, what would you do?
4. Could you develop leisure or other activities as substitutes for work? If so, how could this be done, and when would you want to do this?

E. For those seeking <u>Socialization</u> from work in retirement:
1. What is it about work that helps you meet other people or helps provide a greater sense in you for community or relationships?
2. Are you committed to working to help continue meeting others or is it to avoid dealing with other relationship issues?
3. Could you develop leisure or other activities as substitutes for work to meet your socialization needs? If so, how could this be done, and when would you want to do this?

In Summary:

Based on your diagnosis, what plans could you begin putting in place to better prepare you to make work the most fulfilling it can be for you in retirement.

Concurrently, are there alternative activities that you could begin to initiate in order to replace work in retirement? In considering what you value and what others whose opinions are important to you value, can you imagine ways to make your retirement as fulfilling as possible without working?

[Please return to page 159 to continue reading Chapter 6.]

EXERCISE 3

SATISFIERS AND DISSATISFIERS

Begin by checking off on the first list those items that appeal to you about work (things you'd like to spend time doing in the future), and on the second list those that give you no satisfaction (things you'd rather not do at all). Then follow the instructions for using your answers to summarize your thoughts.

Possible Work Satisfiers

X Items that describe what you like about your work

Work is important and supports my values
Leadership role
Member of a team
Flexible work
Exciting and challenging projects
Managing colleagues
Collegial, supportive environment
Helpful feedback from manager
Using skills and knowledge I've developed
Training and development
Strong team orientation
Being able to independently complete work
Work/life balance
Caring (non-stressful) environment
Values aligned with products/services of organization
Presenting ideas in writing
Giving presentations
Good pay (good benefits)
Having a variety of assignments—minimal repetition
Mentoring and developing others
Opportunities to learn
Networking and building good working relationships
High visibility
Leading edge work and/or using leading edge technology
Influencing others
Need to be to be enterprising, resourceful, etc.
Creativity expected
Learning and being challenged
Travel
Involved in accomplishing important things
Other (please list) _____
_____
_____

Possible Work Dissatisfiers

X Items that describe what you dislike about your work.

Not learning anything new

Workload too heavy to complete at quality level I would like

Repetitious work with little variety

Limited resources for accomplishing difficult goals

People I work with are (too political, unfriendly, unhappy, overworked, etc.)

Rewards are insufficient for working so hard

Promotion opportunities nonexistent

Lack of recognition and/or appreciation

Difficult boss and/or co-workers

Learning new skills not a possibility

No feedback from manager

Stressful environment

Networking opportunities are hard to find

Meetings take up too much time

Too many (not enough) presentations

Lack of administrative or operations support

Management responsibilities are overwhelming (insufficient)

Too much direction from manager – lack of autonomy

Want more (or less) teamwork

Challenges aren't there

No work/life balance – too much work

Constant deadlines

Unstable environment

Travel more (less) than job calls for

Too many tasks I dislike (List) _____

Old technology gets in the way

No training on new technology

Lack of development opportunities

No focus on future

Too much paperwork

Same job for too long – stagnation

Internal politics

Other (please list) _____

_____

_____

Satisfiers and Dissatisfiers

Some Summary Thoughts

There is no perfect job. So it is important that you prioritize the satisfiers and dissatisfiers you've listed. It will help you clarify what trade-offs are possible as you consider various options for job assignments in retirement. It will help you think through what is non-negotiable – particularly in the area of things you may never want to do in a job setting again.

- Review your list of Work Satisfiers and highlight 5-7 that are **most important** to you. These are features you'd like more of in any future work assignment. Consider these when creating your Key Decisions at the end of this chapter.
- Review your list of Work Dissatisfiers and highlight 5-7 that are **most important** to you. These are features you would like less of in any future work assignment. Consider these when creating your Key Decisions at the end of this chapter.

The following exercises will also assist you in identifying work situations that may include those things that are most important to you and eliminate or reduce those kinds of activities or situations that you most dislike. There are also many websites and on-line resources that can help you. The book "Invent Your Retirement," lists on-line resources that can be helpful.

The **RetireRight Center** can be reached at 312-673-3842 if you would like to further discuss your ideas or choices on the telephone or in person. www.retirerightcenter.org

---

[Please return to page 161 to continue reading Chapter 6.]

EXERCISE 4

WORK ENVIRONMENT

From the list of Work Environments below, circle one environment from each group that you prefer over the others.

Working alone	Working with a few people	Working in a large group of people	
Working at home	Working near home	Commuting one-half hour or more to work	
Working indoors	Working outdoors	Working both indoors and outdoors	
Self-employed	Working in a small business	Working in a medium sized organization	Working for a large company
No travel connected with work	Local travel	Some out-of-town travel	Heavy travel
Small town	Medium sized town	Suburb	Large city
Part time work Flexibility for long trips	9-5 hours five days a week Ability to work near second home	Flexible work hours	Heavy schedule with opportunity for overtime
Standing and walking most of the day	Sitting in one place on the job	Both sitting in one place and moving around	
Does not require relocation	May require relocation	Requires frequent relocation	
Extra work must often be done at home	Occasional extra work at home is required	There is never work to be brought home	
Want volunteer work that:	Utilizes talents from my career ----------------------- Offers entirely new kind of work	Makes a difference to individuals ----------------------- Impacts our environment	Brings me visibility ----------------------- Involves large organizational activities
Want work because it provides:	Medical insurance ----------------------- Opportunity to learn	Structure	Investing for retirement

175

List the most important environment items from the above list and in the **Summary of Decisions** at the end of this chapter:

_____   _____

_____   _____

While the above list may help me think about an ideal situation in my future work environment, there are many more things that I may want to consider. Like much of the information in this book, the ideas and exercises presented in this chapter are intended as ways of helping me think and dream about how to make my retirement the best it can be--- for me and the important people in my life. My priorities, values, talents and interests are unique. So are the possibilities for what I see as the ideal environment in which I can thrive in retirement. This is another way of saying that the best use I can make of the tools here is to let them be a starting point, and to spend time considering what I would include in any exercise that is not there not, but is of importance to me.

What else should I consider that is important to me in determining a future occupation, outlet for my talents, or a way to derive an income or some additional cash flow?

_____

[Please return to page 161 to continue reading Chapter 6.]

EXERCISE 5

YOUR VALUES

Each of us brings a unique set of values to what we do each day. They are to each of us what is most important in life, and enter into every decision that we make. Values are not static – they change throughout a lifetime, often without realizing that a gradual shift has taken place.

When making decisions about any big change in your life, it is a good idea to be sure your set of values and the importance of each are clear and strong, and given the appropriate significance in the choices you will be making.

Please see Exercise 2 (page 21) on "Values" in Chapter 1, "Envision Your Ideal Retirement" to gain an overview of what values are important to you at this stage of your career and in your life's journey.

<u>Confirming your values is an important part of making career choices.</u>

List those values that are of utmost importance to you:

A.

B.

C.

D.

E.

[Please return to page 161 to continue reading Chapter 6.]

EXERCISE 6

LIFE'S LESSONS: WORK-LIFE SUCCESSES AND SET-BACKS

In reflecting upon life, many individuals dwell on "What might have been," or decisions they wish they had not made, or unplanned circumstances that occurred causing them considerable unhappiness. It is easy to get into a "negative" mind game.

It is far better to concentrate on one's successes in life, i.e. times that brought you happiness, pride, a sense of accomplishment, recognition, monetary reward, and so forth. It is said that success in life is partially luck and circumstance, but more important is the ability to create circumstances, develop skills, knowledge, and contacts as well as the attitude that fosters success.

In the chapters dealing with work and career, use of leisure time, relationships, and for the good of community, church, or the general good of others, you will be asked to examine the following:

- First, to identify the 2 top key life lessons, typically successes that you had for each review area.
- Second, to identify what you did that brought this life lesson or success into reality.
- Third, particularly in retirement, to identify 2 successes you would love to see occur in each of the key areas of life.
- Fourth, to identify what you could do to bring that future success into reality.

Building on My Work-Life Lessons

This is an opportunity for me to examine or reflect on the successes in my life and then apply it to my future, particularly my future in retirement.

What Was My Greatest Work-Life Lesson or Success?

What Was My 2nd Most Important Work-Life Lesson or Success?

What did I do to create this Lesson?

178

If I had my dream, what would my single greatest future success be?   How would it feel?
How would I feel? Who would share this happiness with me?

What should or could I do to create this future success? When will I start to create this future
success?

[Please return to page 161 to continue reading Chapter 6.]

EXERCISE 7

CAREER COMPETENCIES

Rate yourself in each category by putting an X in the appropriate column:

Give yourself a rating of:

    1 = If you have not actively demonstrated competency on an item. This may mean you don't have that competency or that your current/most recent job doesn't draw upon it.

    2 = If you believe that you have less than operational competency. This may be an area (possibly due to limited opportunity to develop) where you need further development.

    3 = If you believe you are operationally competent.

    4 = If you believe you have a high level of competency and if needed could train others.

If you have a position in mind, please star any competencies you consider to be critical to your success in your desired position.

COMPETENCY	Rating 1	2	3	4
Communicating and Interpersonal Competencies				
Speak clearly and concisely				
Make formal presentations				
Sell ideas				
Justify actions				
Inspire confidence in decisions				
Ask clear, direct questions				
Give clear instructions				
Clarify issues				
Write clearly and concisely				
Listen				
Recognize and overcome blocks to communication				
Deal with diverse views and ambiguity				
Give and receive feedback constructively				
Negotiate to a successful conclusion				
Coach and counsel subordinates				
Conduct interviews				
Lead meetings that achieve their purpose				
Other:				

	Rating			
COMPETENCY	**1**	**2**	**3**	**4**
Conceptual Competencies: Planning and Problem Solving				
Define business unit goals in the context of the organization's goals				
Define problems				
Gather information				
Analyze and evaluate information				
Listen to the ideas of others				
Be decisive in the face of limited information				
Be creative and innovative				
Be logical				
Be realistic				
Be accurate				
Establish strengths for obtaining goals				
Anticipate problems				
Take risks				
Evaluate decisions				
Act on decisions				
Change course if decision is not working				
Take the larger view of working for the good of an organization				
Think in long-range terms				
Exercise good judgment				
Handle ambiguity				
Avoid making premature decisions				
Others:				

Give yourself a rating of:

1 =   If you have not actively demonstrated competency on an item. This may mean you don't have that competency or that your current/most recent job doesn't draw upon it.

2 =   If you believe that you have less than operational competency. This may be an area (possibly due to limited opportunity to develop) where you need further development.

3 =   If you believe you are operationally competent.

4 =   If you believe you have a high level of competency and if needed could train others.

	Rating			
COMPETENCY	**1**	**2**	**3**	**4**
Management and Leadership Competencies				
Organize own work				
Delegate duties and authority				
Follow through on delegated duties				
Interpret policy				
Produce quality work				
Understand and use a variety of management styles				
Develop a cooperative work climate				
Inspire enthusiasm in others				
Establish and enforce performance standards and rules				
Develop people for promotion				
Assess other people accurately				
Be fair and consistent				
Utilize time well				
Coordinate a large number of diverse activities				
Handle change effectively				
Complete objectives within established time frames and cost estimates				
Know personal goals and organization's goals				
Influence others to achieve the organization's goals				
Set priorities and organize work flow				
Others:				

Give yourself a rating of:

1 = If you have not actively demonstrated competency on an item. This may mean you don't have that competency or that your current/most recent job doesn't draw upon it.

2 = If you believe that you have less than operational competency. This may be an area (possibly due to limited opportunity to develop) where you need further development.

3 = If you believe you are operationally competent.

4 = If you believe you have a high level of competency and if needed could train others.

	Rating			
COMPETENCY	1	2	3	4
Personal Competencies: *Emotional Stability and Maturity*				
Take initiative				
Be responsible				
Handle crises and emergencies well				
Work well under pressure				
Resolve personal conflicts with others				
Exercise self control				
Get along well with others				
Assess own strengths and limitations				
Adapt to a changing environment				
Be cooperative				
Take action for self improvement				
Be forthright and open				
Be empathic and understand the feelings of others				
Inspire confidence				
Be enthusiastic				
Be accepting of criticism				
Admit mistakes				
Be flexible				
Be ethical				
Be secure and self confident				
Be respected				
Others:				

Give yourself a rating of:

> 1 = If you have not actively demonstrated competency on an item. This may mean you don't have that competency or that your current/most recent job doesn't draw upon it.
> 2 = If you believe that you have less than operational competency. This may be an area (possibly due to limited opportunity to develop) where you need further development.
> 3 = If you believe you are operationally competent.
> 4 = If you believe you have a high level of competency and if needed could train others.

[Please return to page 162 to continue reading Chapter 6.]

EXERCISE 8

STRENGTHS AND WEAKNESSES

Now that you have focused on your career competencies and given some thought to your own unique set of competencies as well as your talents and experiences, you will find it helpful to summarize.

What are my strengths?
What do I do best? What are my greatest skill areas? What are my talents? List three to five of my top skills below, being sure that they are skills I enjoy using.

1. _____

2. _____

3. _____

4. _____

5. _____

What are My Weaknesses?
What are the areas in which I know I have weaknesses? Are there gaps that might trip me up in landing a job in which I am interested? Are there areas in which I can become more proficient with training or education? And are these areas in which I am interested in developing my ability?

1. _____

2. _____

3. _____

[Please return to page 162 to continue reading Chapter 6.]

SUMMARY OF DECISIONS

PATH 6: WORK IS NO LONGER WORK

Now that you have some background on the topic of WORKING in retirement and have completed the exercises in this chapter, you should have reached some personal decisions which will later become **key (critical) inputs toward completing your final Action Plan in Chapter 8.** Think about what you would like **to do more of,** or perhaps, what you would like to **do less of** in preparing for your most realistic and fulfilling retirement.

You
Decide

What do I want to commit to related to Working in Retirement?

1. I would like to learn how to balance work and other pursuits to achieve the ideal retirement for me.

2. I would like to learn how to manage the changes that will occur when I shift from the usual 9-5 routine to the next stage of my life.

3. I would like to determine what kind of work I would like to do, where I want to work, and the financial considerations of working.

4. I would like to discuss these options with the people most important to me.

What are these **key decisions?**

Key Decision A

_____
_____
_____

Key Decision B

_____
_____
_____

Key Decision C

_____
_____
_____

Other thoughts, questions, ideas, research that needs to be done, etc.:

[Please transfer your decisions into Chapter 8: "Your Action Plan."]

CHAPTER 7

PATH 7: TIME TO DO GOOD... AND FOR GOOD TIMES

"Old age has its pleasures, which, though different, are not less than the pleasures of youth."

W. Somerset Maugham, British novelist and playwright (1874-1965)

In this chapter, you will have the opportunity to:

1. Examine various options relating to your use of leisure time with emphasis upon volunteering and life-long learning.
2. Learn about the changing nature of retirement, i.e. the "New Retirement."
3. Through exercises, you can determine:
   - How you can build on your life's successes.
   - How you want to spend your leisure time including "dream" activities.
   - How you can (1) sharpen your focus in the areas of volunteerism, (2) develop a future life-long learning plan, and (3) plan vacations.

Time for a new identity and restructuring of your time: What do you want out of your retirement?

Leisure…an interesting word that means more to individuals than one would imagine on its surface. The American Heritage Dictionary of American Language defines "Leisure" as "Freedom from time-consuming duties, responsibilities, or activities." It goes on to say: "1. having free time; 2. not employed, occupied, or engaged; 3. unburdened". What does it mean to you (and your spouse, or partner)? Are leisure activities a means of filling in time or are they activities that bring enjoyment to you? Does leisure mean you must also accomplish something? To what extent does it mean both giving of oneself and simultaneously receiving something?

In this section, we will attempt to deal with a subject that some people entering retirement have spent years looking forward to. Is this true for you? Or are you one of those folks who is suddenly tossed into retirement or soon to be retired with no plans for using your leisure time? If this is a situation in which you find yourself, it is not surprising or unusual.

This chapter will assist you in identifying various ways to enjoy your leisure time. This could mean, drawing enjoyment from using your new, available time to your benefit, if not additionally, to the benefit of others. It is not the intention of this book to have you structure all your life's leisure activities. Everyone likes (needs) to take a breather, whether it is a nap, reading a book, going for a walk, completing a crossword puzzle and so forth. We all cherish such time, and hopefully, don't load ourselves with guilt for the time "wasted" on such pursuits.

When it comes to books on retirement planning, not much is written about the art and science of using leisure time. It is fair to say that planning some of your leisure time can result in accomplishing more for yourself and perhaps for others, assuming that such an accomplishment is one of your goals.

Together, let's examine the concept of leisure more closely. In doing so, you will examine your life's commitments and, then, analyze your available time for leisure activities. You will have an opportunity to prioritize those leisure activities you prefer most doing and, finally, identify specific actions you can take to arrange for these most desired elements to be an ongoing part of your life.

You may be thinking, "I have my life well planned and already have arranged my schedules and I know how I want to use my leisure minutes, hours, and days". Congratulations and Bravo! You are certainly fortunate and in the minority when it comes to this subject matter.

Conversely, you may be thinking, "I have been working so hard, or I have been focusing my energy on raising my children (and paying for their education), or taking care of my aging parents, and so forth that I have not thought about using my spare time once my chores and commitments have been attended to." You are not alone in having these thoughts.

Leisure means participating in activities that typically are <u>not</u> routinized or are ones in which you feel obligated to participate. This is not to say that vacations, attending a sporting event or concert series are not planned. Obviously, such activities often require some advanced planning. The distinction is that they occur as a break from your normal daily routine. Once they become routinized or you feel obligated on a scheduled basis, the pure enjoyment of the activity becomes a norm and typically is enjoyed less than when it was originally performed. To repeat, leisure activities are ones:

1. That you look forward to doing;
2. That provide you with a sense of breaking with normal routine;
3. That provide you with the opportunity to either do it or not do it, that is to say, it is completely your decision.

Before exploring different choices, it should be noted that it is recommended that leisure should be a part of everyone's retirement. Notice the words, "be part of", not be the totality or virtually the totality of a person's retirement. What is meant by this?

Recent studies on retirement have found that retirees need a mission or a passion to attain personal fulfillment. Lacking that goal toward achieving something meaningful in one's remaining years may result in a psychological deterioration in a person's physical organs and ultimately in one's overall health.

TIPS

There are two interesting studies that confirm the importance of having goals in retirement. The first is a Harvard study wherein tens of thousands of retirees were studied over a few decades. It was discovered that those retirees that had a strong sense of purpose such as to perform work (as a volunteer or for monetary remuneration), or kept to a routine that focused on achievement, remained physically fit. Those that fell into a routine lifestyle solely of relaxed leisure became more mentally and physically sedentary and hence, physiologically deteriorated quickly, resulting in dying earlier than their more active and intellectually stimulated peers.

Did You Know?

A second study performed at AT&T examined the relationship of time of retirement to the retiree's longevity. Findings indicated that the earlier individuals choose to retire, the greater the length of their lives; inversely, the longer individuals hung onto their jobs, the sooner they perished following their retirement. Why?

Researchers theorize that **those choosing to retire early had plans** to fulfill their lives and were committed to achieving their goals, whereas **those remaining lacked plans**, later became depressed, physically deteriorated, and more quickly died. As an aside, the gender and age of the population most at risk to suicide are males, aged 72. All of this information is not what you may have suspected. Why have it presented here under the topic of leisure?

T I P S

The message to be drawn from these studies…you must have a <u>Balanced Lifestyle</u> which means:

1. <u>Accomplish Something You Desire</u>: Have a mission and plan challenging yourself toward accomplishing something worthwhile, whether it be caring for grandchildren, or building your financial legacy for your children, or volunteering to assist others like driving for "meals on wheels" for the elderly, or working part time, or making or building something new. It is whatever will bring you fulfillment and joy in your ensuing years.
2. <u>Enjoy Yourself</u>: Do activities you can enjoy (and financially afford) whether it is going to the library and reading free magazines there, or watching your favorite sports team, or traveling to new places or to those you love to visit.   Simply stated, enjoy the freedom to choose <u>what (and when) you like</u> to fill your idle time.

To begin this journey, **Exercise 1 (page 201)**: "Building On Life's Lessons: Successes and Set- Backs" in 2 parts: (a) Use of Leisure Time and (b) Volunteering, provides an opportunity for you to think about new ways to build on your previous life experiences so they can bring joy to you and others.

If you stopped and completed Exercise 1, what Lessons or Successes jumped out for you that you think could prove valuable for you in retirement? Now let us move on and see how retirement is evolving and changing for those now entering this period in their lives.

The "New Retirement" Paradigm

Before examining various leisure activities (and our choices are virtually endless, we should again visit this notion of the "New Retirement" paradigm and the old paradigm known as the "Leisure Lifestyle."

Among those nearing retirement age, there is a reluctance to think about how one will manage through what could be 30+ years of retirement. Why? It comes down to one or a combination of any of the following three reasons for procrastination:
1. Individuals are simply too busy.
2. Individuals lack the funds for retiring evidenced by recent studies showing that one-third of Boomers lacked any savings toward retirement. The fact is that the average Boomer has less than $100,000 in savings set aside for retirement, which is completely insufficient to maintain their standard of living unless they continue working.

3. They are fearful. Based on seeing how their parents, grandparents, or others lived in retirement, they fear emulating that type of existence. Or, the thought that they will lose their identity, what made them valuable and unique in their work or profession, may also be another reason to put off planning for retirement.

Apparently, you are interested in doing retirement planning. You know you will someday retire, or you may have a retirement date in mind, or at the very least, you have a sense you will need to cut back on your work and other obligations to free up time to do other things.

You Decide

Doing other things could include working a different job, starting your own business, or in some other way, doing some other major activity in which you can find fulfillment in a new way. Pursuing this new arena of focus will take on the mantle of your new identity distinct and different from your present identity as engineer, draftsperson, plumber, corporate executive, social worker, scientist, or some other work identity.

Your new identity could be as your grandchildren's primary babysitter, or a freelance artist or photographer, antiques restorer, consultant, new business owner---you name it. It will be the "NEW YOU".

Exercises 2 and 3 (pages 204 and 205): "Attitude Toward the Role of Leisure In Your Life" and "Retirement Lifestyle Planning" provide some thought starters for gaining greater fulfillment in use of your unstructured, available time.

If you stopped and completed Exercise 2 and 3, what did you discover about your future use of leisure time? What does it say about you and how effectively you will enter your retirement? Now let's continue examining how retirement evolves over the years for those in retirement.

Retirement Phases: Fast, Medium, Slow

"The person who has lived the most is not the one with the most years but the one with the richest experiences."
Jean Jacques Rousseau, Swiss political philosopher and essayist (1712-1778)

Charlie Davidson, Vice President of Strategy and Business Development for Financial Profiles, wrote the following in an article in *The CPA Journal*, September 2005:

"The behavior of recent retirees suggests a trend that Boomers will likely follow. Their retirement years will become a connected series of phases or speeds that might be labeled

191

fast, medium, and slow. These phases identify the different goals and lifestyles of Boomers after they turn 59. This emerging phenomenon makes sense, considering that many Boomers did not spend their entire working life in one particular job, company, or vocation, as their parents generally did. Many preferred instead to view their work-life as a series of phases.

"Retirees in the 'fast' phase tend to embark on another job as an adventure, sometimes completely different from their previous careers. The primary purpose may be fulfilling lifelong dreams rather than generating current income. Though their new careers may not require the 10-to-12-hour days of their old jobs, many recent retirees find themselves actively filling their time with family, travel, and social activities.

"In the 'medium' phase, seniors may scale back or end their lifestyle-oriented vocation and devote more time to social events, charities, or family. Retirees at this stage, although still active, may want to reduce their commitments and enjoy greater unstructured time. Medical issues become a more significant part of daily life.

"Finally, the 'slow' phase will closely resemble retirement of generations past, where seniors remain close to home most of the time and participate in only a few—but important—social activities, with medical concerns consuming an ever-growing portion of resources."

As the "new you", what will you do as you transition through these stages? In the beginning years of your retirement you may be thinking initially of working for a time in some capacity for the money. This may be only a brief period unless you really need the money. On the other hand, you may wish to work to follow your dream or a long-held "passion," in which case your chief motivation may not be financial remuneration.

You Decide
What is your perceived new identity, the one that replaces your current work title or work function? This new mission, goal, avocation is what is representative of what sociologists and psychologists have called the crux of the "New Retirement". It reflects a set of new routines, a schedule or structure that may occupy a significant percentage of your anticipated waking hours. This new avocation hopefully brings you new opportunities to learn new skills or knowledge, and perhaps, the opportunity to develop new relationships. The need to earn money may or may not be part of the equation, but what is a large portion of the "New Retirement' is the sense that people achieve personal growth. As the famous psychologist Abraham Maslow described this phenomenon, he called it "self-actualization," or the sense of filling a higher calling or personal area of fulfillment.

Some retirees may still have the financial means to pursue a leisure lifestyle. At its optimum, this lifestyle involves living a life devoted to filling one's hours with leisure time activities. It is the Del Webb, Sun City-type existence; where one's days are filled with the routine of playing golf, tennis, or shuffleboard; then going to facilities to work with clay, woodworking, colored glass, building or restoring furniture, playing mahjong, poker, or bridge; then taking in a show at night or dancing and so on. If you see yourself fully engaged and fulfilled in this lifestyle, bravo for you. This is what American culture views as the ideal life for the healthy retiree--a life where a person's past efforts by way of their occupational contributions are viewed as having the most value to society and one where "you earned your way to relaxation" with nothing much more expected of you.

If you cannot foresee a steady stream of leisure days fulfilling your needs, then plan to live in the world of the "New Retiree" and develop a dream around a higher mission or goal for yourself. Along the way, however, you may come to realize that in our American youth culture you will not be encouraged to fulfill your higher calling or be counted on to add value to society. You will be encouraged to relax, enjoy yourself and live out your days out of the mainstream. You will find it difficult being hired as you become older. This may change over time as greater numbers of Boomers retire, but for the short term these attitudes are likely to persist. Battle on and catch your dream. Plan ahead and make it happen!

Getting back to the idea of leisure…what do you like to do in your free time, or put another way, what brings you happiness? Let's examine some choices and self discover what you would like to get from your leisure hours?

Returning to Charlie Davidson's three phases of retirement, what then is his so-called "medium" phase? This is the stage where individuals "may scale back or end their lifestyle-oriented vocation and devote more time to social events, charities, or family." Will you focus on your family, or on your "personal growth"? Let's examine two areas of choice for many retirees: "Volunteerism" and "Lifelong Learning". Let's begin with spending more time and energy as a volunteer. You could be a weekly assigned volunteer at the local food pantry, a staff member at your church or retirement home, the head of the local School Board, or a volunteer for Operation Able. What is your focus?

Volunteering

"It is not enough to merely exist. It's not enough to say, 'I'm earning enough to live and support my family. I do my work well. I'm a good parent.' That's all very well. But you must do something more.

"Seek always to do some good, somewhere. Every person has to seek in his own way to make his own self more noble and to realize his own true worth. You must give some time to your fellow man.

"Even if it's a little thing, do something for those who have need of a man's help, something for which you get no pay but the privilege of doing it. For, remember, you don't live in a world all your own. Your brothers are here too."
Albert Schweitzer, Nobel Peace Prize winner, 1952 (1875-1965)

Most people know what volunteerism means, but to be sure that it is thoroughly understood, here is a definition from Wikipedia, the free encyclopedia:

"**Volunteerism** is the willingness of people to work on behalf of others without the expectation of pay or other tangible gain. Volunteers may have special training as rescuers, guides, assistants, teachers, missionaries, amateur radio operators, writers, and in other positions. But the majority works on an impromptu basis, recognizing a need and filling it, whether it be the dramatic search for a lost child or the mundane giving of directions to a lost visitor. In economics, **voluntary employment** is unpaid employment. It may be done for altruistic reasons, for example charity, as a hobby, community service or vocation, or for the purpose of gaining experience."

?
Did You Know?
Volunteering is not uniquely American, but is truly more heartfelt and responded to in this country than in any other country around the world. Americans have a strong sense of community. The desire to work together and help others derives from the country's founders two centuries ago. "We the People" was built into the fabric of the Constitution at the creation of the U.S. Government. Early settlers felt a resentment toward their former governments' interference in their lives, e.g., their choices of religion, high taxes, etc. Their belief was that they themselves should assist one another, instead of relying on a government to address most of their needs.

The U.S. continues as a country of immigrants who built communities of caring neighbors, churches and communal and fraternal organizations. In Europe, Japan, and other countries, support for those in need was left to governments where allegiance to country and government was viewed as coming before support for the citizenry and their communal needs.

?
Did You Know?
In the U.S. about 61 million people volunteered through or for organizations from September 2005 to September 2006, according to the Bureau of Labor Statistics of the U.S. Department of Labor. The proportion of the population who volunteered was 26.7%. Those that volunteered represented the following percent of their population:

Ages 45-54: 32.2%   Ages 55-64: 30.2%   Ages 65 and beyond: 24.8%.

Those retired or elderly have more time to volunteer so the 24.8% at first appears small; however, this figure includes the truly elderly (aged 90 and above.) Therefore, the commitment to volunteerism is indeed strong in this older population. If you were among this population, would you volunteer to help others?

More than elsewhere in the world, this strong sense of commitment to the "common good" has produced many volunteer organizations, sponsored by philanthropy from corporations and individuals. The strong sense of commitment to community from churches, synagogues and mosques remains strong. Additionally, the Federal U.S. Government supports charitable giving by providing support to individual donors from a tax incentive perspective. "Non-profit" organizations receive special 501(c) (3) status.

This showing of support to the needy by individuals, corporations, and charities was shown in a 1996 survey by Newsweek and NBC News. According to the survey, 40% of the respondents to that survey believe the government should take basic responsibility to help the needy while 31% thought private sectors such as companies and charitable organizations should shoulder the primary support for those needing support. Governments at three levels (Federal, State and local) both directly and indirectly support those in need, but the greater support for the truly needy still falls upon charities, community organizations, and the religious community to meet the need.

Non-profit organizations have in recent times focused on the elderly, immigrants, and certain racial/ethnic communities of need. Volunteers have come to realize the benefits of volunteering which fosters pride, skills, friendships, and knowledge.

You Decide

So, what about it? What about you? To what extent have you built this as an ongoing activity in your plans? Will volunteering find its way on your calendar in retirement? Think about it in larger terms than "this retirement planning is about me and my plans"--think of it in the context of your mental health and how you function in our society.

Here are some organizations where you can search for
VOLUNTEER POSITIONS:

Executive Service Corps Affiliate Network/ www.escus.org
(Provides senior-level consultants for nonprofits, schools, and government agencies)
Score/ www.score.org
(Offer your expertise to help small businesses through nearly 400 chapters)
Service Leader/ www.serviceleader.org
(Click on "for volunteers" for a list of U.S. and international groups)
UN Volunteers/ www.onlinevolunteering.org
(Through the U.N., locate volunteer projects that allow you to work online)
Volunteer Match/ www.volunteermatch.org
(Comprehensive site for searching all types of volunteer slots throughout the U.S.)

"Past the beggar and the suffering walks he, who asks, 'Why, oh God, do you
not do something for these people?' To which God replied, 'I did do
something, I made you.'"
--old Sufi saying

Think about how you can contribute to the needs of others. What could you do? Is it by using your time as well as through your life savings? A review of **Exercise 4 (page 209)**: "Thinking About Volunteering", can provide a deeper sense of how you could add more time and energy to this area of your life.

If you stopped and completed Exercise 4, what did you discover about your attitude and plans for assisting others through actions of volunteering? What did you discover about how you want to be perceived by others in your retirement? Now let's move on again and see how you might continue to increase your knowledge and experience during your retirement years.

Lifelong Learning

"Live as if you were to die tomorrow. Learn as if you were to live forever."
Mahatma Gandhi, major political and spiritual leader of India, known as the "Father" of modern India (1869-1947)

Practical education and academic institutional education programs are a major way for individuals to maintain their mental capabilities as well as their "vim, vigor, and vitality." Education in all forms provides an opportunity to become more worldly, be taken more seriously by others, or perhaps even to be seen by friends or others as very knowledgeable or even "an expert" on a topic of interest. Today, a person can attend classes ranging from cooking classes to non-degree or simple certification university and adult education classes, to programs where one travels with an expert, from "on line" programs over one's computer and/or telephone-in conference arrangements. In addition to the examples just mentioned, there is attendance at Elderhostel traveling programs, church programs and retreats, local library programs, community center programs. There are also programs one can create, such as doing research into various subjects relating to hobbies like studying family history (Genealogy), visiting historical or archeological sites, observing court proceedings, learning about one's favorite sports team, sports figures, famous people, about arts and crafts, etc.

In his book, *Self-Direction for Lifelong Learning: A Comprehensive Guide to Theory and Practice*, Philip Candy writes about the self-directional aspects of controlling one's own personal growth. He presents a careful analysis of the 4 domains of self-directed learning, namely: personal autonomy, willingness to manage one's overall learning endeavors, independent pursuit of learning without formal institutional support or affiliation, and learner-control of instruction. Of course, most of us don't think in these more scholarly terms; we just want to read or study and be entertained, or remain interesting to others.

Exercises 5 and 6 (pages 210 and 211), "Gaining Knowledge and Education: What Would You like To Learn" and "Pursuing Additional Formal Education" are available for you to think in a more structured way about your future personal growth and development.

196

If you stopped and completed Exercises 5 and 6, what did you discover about your plans for your "Personal Growth"? Did you come up with any new approaches to learning? What did you discover about its importance in the scheme of things once you retire? Finally, we move on to other ways to use your leisure time, areas most individuals think of as synonymous with use of leisure time…taking vacations and working on hobbies.

And finally…Vacations, Hobbies, and Final Thoughts

So now we come to the subject that most of us think of when we come to the topic of "retirement""…finding time for vacations and hobbies. By now, if you have taken the challenges of completing earlier chapters and exercises, you could be thinking, "Where will I have the time for hobbies and travel, what with focusing on health and exercise, possible work, volunteering, life-long learning, and so forth?" You will no doubt find time for vacations and hobbies or other leisure time activities.

 Exercises 7 and 8 (pages 212 and 215), "Traveling Vacations" and "Examining Hobbies and Leisure Time Activities," will help you "round out" and perhaps give some structure to your remaining daytime hours. Remember the notion of <u>Life Balance</u>.

In determining how vacations, travel and hobbies fit into your balanced lifestyle, what have you concluded by completing Exercises 7 and 8? Did you have any surprises or discoveries that will help you plan more thoughtfully in this area of your retirement life?

Did you discover that what you thought of as a hobby (the traditional golf, gardening, doing needlepoint, stamp or coin collecting, etc.) proved to take less or more of your planned time than you would have guessed? Did you find that travel, seeing relatives and friends, volunteering, and caring for others could take much more or less time than you anticipated? Did you learn that what you thought were "not on your radar" will actually take quite a bit of time in retirement and, thus, replace the more conventional definition of a "hobby" for which you will find enjoyment?

Finally, there is a growing trend among vacationers who want to add "doing good" to their travel itinerary. Volunteers, including a significant number of those who are already retired and have more time, actually pay to travel with a mission or charitable agency to work in countries that need help. At the forefront of this trend are older Americans who have the money to travel to far-flung places. The world is full of indigent communities that need the passion, adventurous spirit and life experience that older Americans have to really make a difference in these far-flung locations. You can stay a week to a year living with a local family in their home, or in a tent in the jungle, or in a Western-style hotel. The success of your sojourn will depend in large part on the sponsor organization's in-country approach and how adventurous and energetic you really are. As an example, for prices ranging anywhere from hundreds to thousands of dollars, you can:

- Help care for orphans in Africa caused by the AIDs epidemic;
- Help care for abandoned children in Romania foster-care facilities;
- Band and care for gibbons in Madagascar or Borneo;
- Construct rain-forest paths in the Amazon or houses in New Orleans;
- Unearth ancient settlements or archeological ruins in Mexico, Turkey or Jordan;
- Harvest grain in Tibet;
- Work on a collective farm (Kibbutz) in Israel; or
- Teach English in Peru or Guatemala.

Here are some of the sources that may help you decide if you want to "voluntour:"
- **Cross- Cultural Solutions** (offer work and cultural-exchange opportunities in 12 nations—800-380-4777; www.crossculturalsolutions.org);
- **Volunteers for Peace** (802-259-2759) www.vfp.org;
- **Global Volunteers** (has programs in the U.S. and 18 other countries —800-422-487-1047; www.globalvolunteers.org);
- **Habitat for Humanity** (sends teams around the world through its Global Village Program—800-422-4828; www.habitat.org);
- **Projects Abroad** (does everything from conservation work to archaeology projects in 20 countries—888-839-3535);
- **United Planet** (runs projects in over 50 nations—800-292-2316; www.unitedplanet.org); i to i (800-985-4864) www.itoi.com); and
- The guidebook: *Volunteer Vacations* (Chicago Review Press, 2006) by Bill McMillon, Doug Cutchins, and Anne Geissinger.

In conclusion, take your time in completing the next chapter's "Action Plan." Your investment in doing so will find its way into returns that only you can imagine and bring into reality. Remember that retirement is just another career change on life's journey. How you plan it and then use your remaining days probably will become more important than any job you ever held. Be all you can be and do all you can do. If you read much of this book and completed many of the exercises, you are well on your way to ensuring your retirement will be meaningful, fun and exciting, and most of all, both rewarding and fulfilling.

"There's a difference between interest and commitment. When you're interested in doing something, you do it only when circumstances permit. When you're committed to something, you accept no excuses, only results."
Anonymous

CHAPTER 7

PATH 7: TIME TO DO GOOD… AND FOR GOOD TIMES

EXERCISES

If you have not already done so, now is your opportunity to complete the following exercises which will assist you in making decisions related to examining your future use of leisure time, finding fulfillment, spending time volunteering or traveling, taking opportunities to expand your knowledge, and so forth, thereby, hopefully helping you to consider dealing with alternative situations and opportunities.

Exercise 1 (in 2 parts): Building On Life's Lessons: Successes or Set-Backs
    Part A: Building On Life's Lessons through Use of Leisure Time
    Part B: Building On Life's Lessons Relating to Volunteering in Community,
            Church or other Venues

Exercise 2: Attitude toward the Role of Leisure in Your Life

Exercise 3: Retirement Lifestyle Planning

Exercise 4: Thinking About Volunteering

Exercise 5: Gaining Knowledge and Education: What Would You Like To Learn?

Exercise 6: Pursuing Additional Formal Education

Exercise 7: Traveling Vacations

Exercise 8: Examining Hobbies and Leisure Time Activities

At the conclusion of the exercises is a "**Summary of Decisions**" page, which will allow you to think through some of the thoughts and ideas you have been gathering in completing this chapter. Please take some time to evaluate the information you have both reviewed and created, and then summarize some key points in writing that you would like to pursue in putting together your final action plan in this book's last chapter, "**Your Action Plan…Putting It All Together.**"

EXERCISE 1

BUILDING ON MY LIFE'S LESSONS: MY SUCCESSES OR, PERHAPS, SET-BACKS IN LEISURE TIME AND IN VOLUNTEERING

In reflecting upon life, many individuals dwell on "What might have been," or decisions they wish they had not made or unplanned circumstances that occurred causing them unhappiness. It is easy to get into a "negative" mind game.

It is far better to concentrate on one's successes in life, i.e. times that brought you happiness, pride, a sense of accomplishment, recognition, monetary reward, and so forth. It is said that success in life is partially luck and circumstance, but more important is the ability to create circumstances, develop skills, knowledge, and contacts as well as the attitude that fosters success.

Instructions for this Exercise:

First, you will identify the 2 top key "life lessons," typically successes that you had for the following 2 review areas:

- Part A: Use of your leisure time
- Part B: Volunteering in community, church or other venues

Second, you will identify what <u>you did</u> that brought this life lesson or success into reality.

Third, you will identify 2 successes you would love to see occur in each of these key areas of your life, particularly in retirement.

Fourth, you will identify what you <u>could do</u> to bring that future success into reality.

PART A: BUILDING ON LIFE'S LESSONS THROUGH USE OF LEISURE TIME

This is an opportunity for me to examine or reflect on the successes in my life in my leisure time and then apply them to my future, particularly my future in retirement.

What Was My Greatest Lesson or Success relating to the use of leisure time in the past?

What Was My 2nd Greatest Leisure Time Lesson or Success?

What did I do to cause these Lessons or Success?

If I had my dream, what would my single greatest future success be? How would it feel? How would I feel? Who would share this happiness with me?

What should or could I do to create this future success? When would I need to begin to work on this?

PART B: BUILDING ON LIFE'S LESSONS RELATING TO VOLUNTEERING IN COMMUNITY, CHURCH OR OTHER VENUES

This is an opportunity for me to examine or reflect on the successes in my life pertaining to my volunteer work and then apply them to my future, particularly my future in retirement.

What Was the Greatest Lesson or Success I derived from volunteering?

What Was My 2nd Greatest Lesson or Success?

What did I do to cause these Lessons or Success?

If I had my dream, what would my single greatest future success be?   How would it feel? How would I feel? Who would share this happiness with me?

What should or could I do to create this future success? When would I need to begin to work on this?

[Please return to page 190 to continue reading Chapter 7.]

EXERCISE 2

ATTITUDE TOWARD THE ROLE OF LEISURE IN YOUR LIFE

To what extent do you gain satisfaction or fulfillment from the following leisure-type activities?

Leisure Activity	To a Great Extent	To Some Extent	Little	Not at All
Opportunity:				
To grow and study				
To relax and unwind				
To gain serenity				
To contemplate/reflect				
To build new skills				
To gain new knowledge				
To create new works/artistry				
To be with others I like				
To meet new challenges				
To build new relationships				
To investigate new interests				
To watch sporting events/TV				
To venture into new terrain, i.e., to experience new things				
To participate in sports				
To use/experience new physical or mental personal aspects of myself				
To acquire new material things				
To see new places				
To volunteer my time				
To teach, mentor, coach				
To address a "passion" or strong area of interest				

Which of these do you wish to increase?

What does use of leisure time say about you?

[Please return to page 191 to continue reading Chapter 7.]

EXERCISE 3

RETIREMENT LIFESTYLE PLANNING

How do I want to spend my leisure time, (even if I need to work to make ends meet)?

With which of the following do I see myself spending more or less time?

For each statement below, mark each activity as to whether you realistically expect to spend more or less time doing each of the following activities:

- Volunteering

- Visiting with others I like

- Shopping for enjoyment

- Exercising

- Helping children/grandchildren

- Vacationing/sightseeing/traveling

- Simply relaxing, i.e. pleasure reading, sleeping, watching TV or being on my computer networking

- Learning new things by reading, attending programs/classes, attending cultural events, learning from tapes, videos, etc.

- Mentoring

- Tutoring

- Working on an organization's board

- Taking care of animals

- Narrating "Audio Books" for the publisher or for organizations that assist the blind

- Taking part in political action activities

- Other activities (indicate them)

Now take the leisure items shown above for which you plan to spend more time and decide how this will occur. To do this you will first need to decide how you will reduce the number of items and/or the time spent on other more demanding activities. For each activity you wish to reduce, take that item and decide what needs to change to facilitate your reducing time on that activity?

List the activities below that you wish to minimize. What are you willing to change on each activity (time spent or eliminate completely, so you can spend more time on the activities you want to spend more time on)?

First Activity that I want to minimize and how I will do that:

Second Activity that I want to minimize and how I will do that:

Third Activity that I want to minimize and how I will do that:

Now, for those items you identified that you want to spend more time on, identify what you will need to do to build your list of "dream" activities:

- Do you need to contact others to set up plans? Whom?
- Do you need to purchase equipment, time, transportation, and so forth? When?
- Do you have to schedule the activity? How?
- Do you have to set aside money for it? How much?

Take each "dream" activity and plan it, using the four bulleted questions above. When will you carry out these plans?

Dream Activity 1:

Dream Activity 2:

Dream Activity 3:

Dream Activity 4:

Finally, for the fun of it, identify the extent to which you will derive happiness/fulfillment from each of these dream activities. Which ones will provide?

- A sense of pride?

- A sense of achievement?

- A sense of simple enjoyment?

- A sense of commitment?

- A sense of power or control?

- An opportunity to boast?

You decide...You plan and You enjoy!

[Please return to page 191 to continue reading Chapter 7.]

EXERCISE 4

THINKING ABOUT VOLUNTEERING

Many individuals in retirement find a great deal of reward comes from the opportunity to volunteer in order to help others in need. They find they receive the following types of satisfaction from performing such service: Rate each item as High/ Medium/ or Low

Item	High	Medium	Low
1. Pride in helping friends, those needy, or their community or church.			
2. The opportunity to meet with others and establish relationships.			
3. Sometimes, the chance to make some "pocket change" for themselves.			
4. To financially support an organization in need of money, food or other charity.			
5. The possibility of achieving something important or supporting a cause.			
6. To fill an urgent need on an emergency basis.			
7. To provide leadership or training to those less skilled or knowledgeable.			
8. To simply keep occupied.			
9. To get out of the house as a break or to avoid too much togetherness at home.			
10. Other needs you might have for volunteering:			

Which of the above reasons address your needs? If you were asked to rank order your reasons for volunteering, which would rank highest, second and third highest for you?

How much time would you anticipate volunteering? Would it be a few hours a week or several mornings a week? Could you afford to give more time than that?

Let's take a look at various organizations for which people volunteer.
Which would be the top 2 or 3 organizations that you would see yourself assisting?

Volunteering, you decide where:
- At Church, Synagogue, Mosque?
- As a worker on a campaign?
- In the school as an instructor?
- At a nursing home or hospital?
- As a baby-sitter?
- At a service center or phone bank?
- At the YMCA, the fire department, or similar organization?
- At the local women's shelter or food pantry?

On a (school or election) Board?
As a tour guide?
As an EMT?
As a coach or mentor?
As a driver?
In a school as an instructor?

Whom would you need to call to arrange to start helping?
[Please return to page 196 to continue reading Chapter 7.]

EXERCISE 5

GAINING KNOWLEDGE AND EDUCATION

What would you like to Learn

Retirement is an opportunity to learn about new things…both information and facts, as well as how to do things. Below are examples of more formal and less formal learning events. List out what you would like to learn:

Examples of Formal Learning Opportunities

- Study comparative religions
- Learn about my ancestry…study genealogy
- Get my teaching certification to teach math and science
- Get my Flight Pilot's License
- Study military history
- Learn coaching/mentoring skills
- Complete my doctorate in Psychology
- Learn how to sail
- Take piano lessons

My TOP 3 Formal Learning Initiatives

1. _____

2. _____

3. _____

Examples of Informal Learning Opportunities

- Learn to build furniture
- Examine how to rent a property in Tuscany
- Attend cooking classes to make a soufflé
- Study how to win at poker
- Evaluate how I can become a novelist
- Join an Investment Club

My Top 3 Informal Learning Initiatives

1. _____

2. _____

3. _____

[Please return to page 196 to continue reading Chapter 7.]

EXERCISE 6

PURSUING ADDITIONAL FORMAL EDUCATION

Pursuing formal education does not mean necessarily pursuing a certification or a degree from an accredited university or college. It could mean attending classes just to learn and be with other learners. It could also mean going to adult education classes at a neighboring high school or through a park district, taking lessons or tutoring, or scheduling a program through an organization like Elderhostel.

In a previous exercise, "What I Would Like To Learn", you were asked to identify a preliminary list of "My TOP 3 Formal Learning Initiatives". What did you indicate?

1. _____
2. _____
3. _____

As you look forward to your remaining working years and then retirement, what is the purpose of this additional formal education?

1. To make me more employable or promotable?
2. To make more money?
3. To strengthen my skills to perform an activity?
4. To simply expand my knowledge or to broaden my horizons?
5. For other reasons that include _____.

How much time are you committing to pursuing this additional learning? Have you built this plan into your calendar?

How much money have you set aside, or are committed to spending for this education? If you haven't got the finances, where will the money come from and when?

With whom do you need to discuss this to make it a reality?

[Please return to page 196 to continue reading Chapter 7.]

EXERCISE 7

TRAVELING VACATIONS

There are several factors that affect the choices one has related to vacation planning:

1. Money Available	4. Who/What One Wants to See
2. Time available	5. One's Means/Methods of Travel
3. One's physical health	6. Voluntouring (Combining Travel and Volunteer Work)

Consider each of the items below in relation to your travel needs and desires. Check the items that make sense to you.

Money Available:

1. Money is not an issue preventing my taking pre-determined vacations.
2. Taking nice vacations is very important and can be afforded based on money (frequent flier miles) having been set aside.
3. Affordability is a major consideration in determining vacation accessibility (so some occasional more expensive and some less expensive vacations can be planned).
4. It is possible to take an occasional inexpensive trip or trips.
5. Insufficient funds prevent my taking vacations involving travel unless I stay at friends or relatives.
6. Insufficient funds prevent me from traveling from my home location.

Time Available:

1. How often can you travel? Monthly? Quarterly? Once a year? Twice a year?
2. When you travel, how long do you prefer being away? For single day trips only? For a few days? For a week? For several weeks at a time? For an extended stay (state how long _____)?

One's Physical Health:

1. My health (and my travel companion's health) is excellent and encourages me to take vacations that involve or require a good degree of exercise (i.e. skiing, climbing, bicycling, backpacking, hiking, kayaking, adventuring, etc.).
2. My health (and my travel companion's health) is such that I am not inhibited from performing moderate exercise (climbing stairs, walking long distances, climbing hills, dealing with high or low temperatures, carrying 20-30 pounds of luggage, etc.).
3. My health (and my travel companion's health) is such that general air and ground travel, cruising, and moderate walking and occasional stair climbing are okay.
4. My health (and my travel companion's health) is such that it is no longer pleasant to travel by air and climbing and walking are becoming laborious.
5. Occasional travel or visiting is a possibility, provided I receive assistance.

Check those items that make sense to you.

Who and What Do I Want To See:

1. To see my immediate family, children and grandchildren
2. To see my friends
3. To travel abroad
4. To travel locally, within 50 miles for museums, art fairs, state fairs, sporting events, concerts, shows, parks and nature trails, etc.
5. To travel across this country
6. To stay at my second residence
7. To be at beautiful resorts
8. To attend specific events…sporting events, alumni gatherings, etc.
9. To go to and stay at the beach, mountain retreat, hostel, retreat (monastery) center
10. To provide a voluntary service…Habitat for the Humanities, the Peace Corp., etc.
11. To travel on the seas…cruises, sailing one's ship.

One's Means/Method of Travel:

1. By car
2. By RV
3. By air
4. By ship
5. By train
6. By a tour (educational, travel, camping)

"Voluntouring":

1. Working in an orphanage
2. Working at an archeological site
3. Creating water purification systems for a remote village
4. Teaching in an impoverished area
5. Other

Summarizing One's Plans: Based On Considerations Checked Above, Consider Using the Chart On the Next Page To Plan Travel and Vacationing Over Your First 5 Retirement Years (Or the Next 5 Years If Already Retired)?

TRAVEL AND VACATION PLANNING:

YEAR 1 PLANS	1st Quarter:	2nd Quarter:	3rd Quarter:	4th Quarter:
• WHAT • WHERE • HOW MANY $$ • WITH WHOM				
YEAR 2 PLANS	1st Quarter:	2nd Quarter:	3rd Quarter:	4th Quarter:
• WHAT • WHERE • HOW MANY $$ • WITH WHOM				
YEAR 3 PLANS	1st Quarter:	2nd Quarter:	3rd Quarter:	4th Quarter:
• WHAT • WHERE • HOW MANY $$ • WITH WHOM				
YEAR 4 PLANS	1st Quarter:	2nd Quarter:	3rd Quarter:	4th Quarter:
• WHAT • WHERE • HOW MANY $$ • WITH WHOM				
YEAR 5 PLANS	1st Quarter:	2nd Quarter:	3rd Quarter:	4th Quarter:
• WHAT • WHERE • HOW MANY $$ • WITH WHOM				

[Please return to page 197 to continue reading Chapter 7.]

EXERCISE 8

EXAMINING HOBBIES AND LEISURE TIME ACTIVITIES

Changing from a structured to a fully or significantly unstructured lifestyle is a major transition for many individuals who have spent the preponderance of their time in work-related activities. It takes time to adjust to a new schedule of activities.

How do you see this transition evolving for you? Will it be simple or difficult for you? To assist you in determining how you will choose to use your new-found unstructured time, please complete the following. Try to get to 5 items in each set below, or if you can arrive at more than 5, narrow the list to your top 5 choices:

I see myself taking part in more of the following:

- _____
- _____
- _____
- _____
- _____

(Examples: visits with friends, attending more church meetings, seeing concerts or the movies, watching my grandkids' sporting events, attending Weight Watcher meetings, bridge tournaments, or square dancing sessions.)

I see myself creating more of the following:

- _____
- _____
- _____
- _____
- _____

(Examples: creating a new business venture, writing my memoirs, composing a musical, new works of art, building new furniture, constructing a darkroom for developing my pictures, or putting together new food recipes)

I see myself learning more of the following:

- _____
- _____
- _____
- _____
- _____

(Examples: how to play bridge, to sail or to fly a plane, study more about comparative religions, how to invest in stocks like a pro, to improve my golf game, or learn what my children's days with their children are like.)

I see myself participating in more of the following:

- _____
- _____
- _____
- _____
- _____

(Examples: intramural softball, travel with my life partner, becoming active in political events, touring with others around our historic sites, being on the church advisory council, marching in our annual parades, joining the local stamp club, reading to elders, staging the local theater group's new productions.)

I see myself celebrating more of the following:

- _____
- _____
- _____
- _____
- _____

(examples: birthdays/weddings, family events, alumni events, sporting events, (play-offs and championships), political victories, neighborhood gatherings, holiday events at the Rotary or VFW post, bake-off competitions, the revues of a new stage play, our wedding anniversary, the repair of my car, the redecorating of our home, religious holidays, or the launch of a new business.)

I see myself achieving or taking on more of the following:

- _____
- _____
- _____
- _____
- _____

(Examples: fishing, hiking and walking, babysitting, house cleanup and redecorating, travel to our second home, achieving my passion for measuring/reporting weather changes to the government, completing that college certification, teaching, counseling for Big Brothers, running our annual Rotary event, building that parade float, or hosting two exchange students next year.)

I see myself relaxing more in the following ways:

- _____
- _____
- _____
- _____
- _____

(Examples: listening to my CDs, swimming every day, needle pointing, working crossword puzzles and Sudoku puzzles, playing with my grandchildren, playing golf, fishing, working on my coin collection, going for a walk, reading all those books I set aside, dabbling in stock trading, watching TV, attending movies once per week, taking naps, whittling, telephoning my friends, going out to breakfast, or simply doodling.)

I see myself spending some money or investing in the following leisure activities:

- _____
- _____
- _____
- _____
- _____

(Examples: using my frequent flier miles for that New Zealand trip, buying new beads for making jewelry bracelets, hiring a part-time electrician to assist me in my work building a finished basement, purchasing a new dog and pet supplies, buying a new trail bike, buying a new recreation vehicle, purchasing season opera tickets, joining the local golf club, buying that new computer and wideband and hook-up for internet blogging and gaming, or buying that new cookware set.)

What are 4 key discoveries that you learned about yourself and your ability to either fill or utilize your future leisure time?

1st Discovery	
2nd Discovery	
3rd Discovery	
4th Discovery	

Based on the chart above, how comfortable do you feel with this available time use?

Based on the chart above, is there anything you should plan to do differently or more of?

Based on the chart above, is there anyone you should talk to about this and when?

[Please return to page 197 to continue reading Chapter 7.]

SUMMARY OF DECISIONS

PATH 7: TIME TO DO GOOD...AND FOR GOOD TIMES

Now that you have some background on the topic of "**Time To Do Good and For Good Times**" and have completed the exercises in this chapter, you should have reached some personal decisions which will later become **key (critical) inputs toward completing your final Action Plan in Chapter 8.** Think about what you would like **to do more of,** or perhaps, what you would like to **do less of** in preparing for your most realistic and fulfilling retirement. Consider in what capacity you see yourself changing your lifestyle and actions in the future and why.

☞ **You Decide** What do I want to commit to working on related to my vision of a successful retirement?

1. I would like to further evaluate various options relating to my use of leisure time with emphasis upon volunteering and life-long learning.

2. Having learned more about the changing nature of retirement, i.e. the "New Retirement" paradigm, I would like to further clarify a new identity, which includes structuring my time in the coming years.

3. I would like to follow up on the exercises sharpening my plans for "dream" activities, including perhaps, among other areas, doing more volunteering, developing a future life-long learning plan, and planning vacations and travel.

4. I would like to work on determining how leisure time can be fulfilling to me and assess how much time I wish to dedicate pursuing leisure time (non-working) activities.

What are your **key decisions?**

Key Decision A

_____

_____

Key Decision B

_____

_____

Key Decision C

_____

_____

Other thoughts, questions, ideas, research that needs to be done, etc.
Please transfer your decisions into Chapter 8 (Page 238): "Your Action Plan"

CHAPTER 8

YOUR ACTION PLAN

Putting It All Together

"Climb ev'ry Mountain,
Search high and low,
Follow every byway,
Every path you know.

Climb ev'ry mountain,
Ford every stream,
Follow every rainbow,
Till you find your dream."

You can make it happen

You Decide Consolidating all your individual plans from the other chapters in the book into a framework for action is a desirable goal. At the same time, coming up with an overarching plan that encompasses all the elements that will create the future style of retirement that you dream of is well worth pursuing…but clearly it is not an easily developed initiative. Nevertheless, **you can successfully do it!** This is because, if you have completed the exercises in the previous chapters, you have all the ingredients **TO MAKE IT HAPPEN!** You can realize your dream by making the plan and by having the discipline to pursue it; you gain the reality on a step-by-step basis. Much like losing weight, improving one's golf game, saving money, arriving at a travel destination In all these and similar circumstances, reaching your end-goals requires the following:

1. Clarifying your end goal(s) and visualizing it (them) as attainable.
2. Identifying small incremental steps that you will take to build one upon another toward achieving the larger end goal.
3. Understanding that, like driving to a destination, with construction projects, missing street signs, accidents and other situations that may drive one off course, an individual has to make adjustments, always keeping the destination in mind and focusing on getting there. Reaching a set of goals is never a straight line of success.

So now, let's put it all together and make it happen.

Chapter 1 -- Path 1: Envision You Ideal Retirement

In Chapter 1, you were asked a series of questions which may have helped you discover your dreams for the future. Based on your answers, you probably were led to examine the other chapters that continued your inquiry into current activities and desires for your retirement lifestyle. Your responses to the *Summary of Decisions* at the end of each chapter may help you in putting together your Action Plan.

Wake Up and Dream

To get you started in developing your Action Plan, please complete the following word or visual pictures of your planned retirement over time:

<u>1 Year After Retirement</u>:   **Write below, what would my typical retirement picture look like? How would I achieve my biggest goals?**

_____

_____

_____

_____

_____

_____

_____

_____

_____

_____

_____

_____

_____

_____

Are there areas that remain sketchy for me? What can be done to clarify them further? List out who it would be helpful to speak with in order to gain greater clarity on choices and actions?

_____
_____
_____
_____
_____
_____
_____
_____
_____
_____

7 Years After Retirement:

7 Years is usually tied to the "7 year Itch"…The time when a person is in need of making changes. On that basis, please draw a number of word pictures portraying what my life would be like at the following milestone, i.e. what will be different and unique from the previous picture?

<u>7 years after retirement</u>. Write below:

What are some surprises or new discoveries that I came up with? What are the implications of these discoveries?

_____
_____
_____
_____
_____
_____
_____
_____

14 Years After Retirement: **What will be different and unique from the previous picture?**

Write Below:

How did I project my retirement evolving over time? In assessing changes over time, did I consider in my projections that my health might change? What did I find were areas that need further refinement or action to insure a successful retirement at various stages in my life?

_____
_____
_____
_____
_____
_____
_____
_____
_____
_____

What are some surprises or new discoveries that I came up with? What are the implications of these discoveries?

_____
_____
_____
_____
_____
_____
_____

Now, examine the 3 "Key Decisions" I noted on the "Summary of Decisions" page at the conclusion of Chapter 1—Path 1 (page 32.) To which 3 Key Decisions did I commit? Think about the extent to which these 3 Key Decisions are built into my thoughts above. Are there other thoughts, ideas, research, that I noted in Chapter 1 that need to be pursued beyond what I wrote above in this Action Plan? Do I need to take any additional action?

_____
_____
_____
_____
_____
_____
_____
_____
_____
_____

Chapter 2 – Path 2: The Financial Picture…Making it a Masterpiece

In the chapter pertaining to financial planning, there were three exercises examining: (1) your level of knowledge of financial matters, and (2) the extent to which you have clarity about your financial circumstances and (3) whether you are "on the same page" with the other important people in your life related to planning and knowing your future financial circumstances.

Please answer the following questions in order to develop more insight or to confirm that you have your financial "house in order" so that you will be able to meet your financial retirement goals.

How would I describe my level of knowledge relating to financial matters? What would I see myself doing (and be committed to doing) in order to increase my current financial knowledge? Who should I see on these matters? When?

_____
_____
_____
_____
_____
_____
_____
_____
_____
_____

Do I know the amount of money needed to live the retirement lifestyle I described above? If not, what do I need to do to get a clearer picture of this? Who could help me? When can I see these individuals in order to get this clarified?

_____
_____
_____
_____
_____
_____

Once retired, can I restrict my portfolio withdrawals to an amount that will last throughout my life (and the life of my life partner)? If I don't know the facts surrounding this, what needs to be done? If I know there is a shortfall, how will I fill the gap? What do I need to do to get a clearer picture of this? Who could help me? When can I see myself getting all this clarified?

_____
_____
_____
_____
_____
_____
_____
_____
_____

Do I recall completing the exercise called the "Financial PEACE Exercise?" In that exercise, I identified a number of actions that remain undone. In some cases, it is appropriate that they have not been done, but some other items clearly need to be completed. List those items that I believe need to be completed and identify when I plan to pursue them:

<u>Item To Be Completed</u>   <u>When</u>   <u>Who Else Needs to Be Involved</u>

1. _____
2. _____
3. _____
4. _____
5. _____
6. _____
7. _____
8. _____
9. _____

Now, examine the 3 "Key Decisions" I noted on the "Summary of Decisions" page at the conclusion of Chapter 2 – Path 2 (page 72.) To which 3 Key Decisions did I commit? Think about the extent to which these 3 Key Decisions are built into my thoughts above. Are there other thoughts, ideas, research, that I noted in Chapter 2 that need to be pursued beyond what I wrote above in this Action Plan? Do I need to take any additional action?

_____
_____
_____
_____
_____

Chapter 3 – Path 3: Keeping in Shape

After examining my current health situation, as well as the health condition of those that would directly impact my future ability to live the retirement lifestyle that I desire, what key points did I discover?

1. _____
   _____
2. _____
   _____
3. _____
   _____
4. _____
   _____
5 _____
   _____

Based on the facts above, what 5 major health-related activities do I have to address to insure I have a secure, satisfying retirement?

Activity To Be Completed	When	Who Else Needs to be Involved

1. _____
   _____
   _____
2. _____
   _____
   _____
3. _____
   _____
   _____
4. _____
   _____
   _____
5. _____
   _____
   _____

Now, examine the 3 "Key Decisions" I noted on the "Summary of Decisions" page at the conclusion of Chapter 3 – Path 3 (page 101.) To which 3 Key Decisions did I commit? Think about the extent to which these 3 Key Decisions are built into my thoughts above. Are there other thoughts, ideas, research, that I noted in Chapter 3 that need to be pursued beyond what I wrote above in this Action Plan? Do I need to take any additional action?

Chapter 4 – Path 4: Being At Home

In the chapter "Being At Home", I had the opportunity to examine the conditions under which I currently live, i.e. my happiness with my current residence, its physical condition, what needs to be done to make it more livable, valuable, and perhaps saleable (if this applies); how my housing needs may change over time; my desires for relocation; and the costs inherent in these choices. In thinking through these matters, what did I learn and decide to do?

1._____
_____
_____
_____
2._____
_____
_____
3._____
_____
_____
_____

In examining my housing needs <u>in the early years of retirement</u> (choose a timeframe…5, 7, 10, 12 years), what do I believe is reasonably realistic for my plans for future retirement residency, i.e. living in my present home, refurbishing, major renovation, downsizing, living in two residences (North and South), renting, living abroad part of the year, etc? To what extent do I have to set aside monies or make other changes toward achieving these plans? How much money is needed? Whom do I have to speak to about this, and when do I have to take action to make my plans a reality? List my thoughts below:

_____
_____
_____
_____
_____
_____
_____

What do I believe is a reasonably realistic plan for my future retirement residency in the early years of retirement?

_____
_____
_____
_____
_____
_____
_____

To what extent do I have to set aside monies to achieve these plans? How much money is needed?

_____
_____
_____
_____
_____
_____
_____

What other actions are required toward achieving my plans? Whom do I have to speak to about this, and when do I have to take action to make my plans a reality?

_____
_____
_____
_____
_____
_____

In projecting my housing needs further into my retirement (choose a timeframe…12-15 years or later following initial entry into retirement), what do I believe is a reasonably realistic plan to identify and plan changes to my future retirement residency? Without going into detail about these possible changes, what might be a few logical scenarios that could alternatively occur? What could I do to plan for these possibilities? Who could I turn to for assistance or with whom should I eventually discuss these potential occurrences? List some of my thoughts below:

_____
_____
_____
_____
_____
_____

What do I believe are some potentially realistic options for my future retirement residency in the later years of retirement?

_____
_____
_____
_____
_____

To what extent will I be financially secure to maintain a place to live in the later years of my retirement? Will I need a reverse mortgage, sell my principal residence, use my savings to relocate closer to family members, or move into an independent and/or assisted-living facility? When and whom could I turn to for assistance or with whom should I eventually discuss these potential occurrences?

_____
_____
_____
_____
_____

Now, examine the 3 "Key Decisions" I noted on the "Summary of Decisions" page at the conclusion of Chapter 4 -- Path 4 (page 123.) To which 3 Key Decisions did I commit? Think about the extent to which these 3 Key Decisions are built into my thoughts above. Are there other thoughts, ideas, research, that I noted in Chapter 4 that need to be pursued beyond what I wrote above in this Action Plan? Do I need to take any additional action?

_____
_____
_____
_____
_____

Chapter 5 – Path 5: Vitalizing Relationships

Much of what life is all about is how individuals, in this case…you… relate to others, especially those you consider most important to your happiness. In addition, there is the important attribute of obligation to others, whether your obligation is to immediate family members, friends, and/or others, perhaps in your community. In the chapter titled, "Vitalizing Relationships", you examined how these relationships currently exist and how they could or should be changed following entry into retirement?

What did I determine about my important relationships? Which relationships do I project will remain unchanged? Which will change considerably? What plans do I need to make to evolve my relationships? Choose 8 of my most important relationships and decide what (if anything) needs to be done to change or develop each relationship:

Relationship with:	What Needs to Change:	How to Bring About a Change:
1.		
2.		
3.		
4.		
5.		
6.		
7.		
8.		

Now, examine the 3 "Key Decisions" I noted on the "Summary of Decisions" page at the conclusion of Chapter 5 – Path 5 (page 152.) To which 3 Key Decisions did I commit? Think about the extent to which these 3 Key Decisions are built into my thoughts above. Are there other thoughts, ideas, research, that I noted in Chapter 5 that need to be pursued beyond what I wrote above in this Action Plan? Do I need to take any additional action?

_____
_____
_____
_____
_____

Chapter 6 – Path 6: Work Is No Longer Work

In the chapter titled "Work is No Longer Work", you were provided with an opportunity to examine the notion of working in retirement. As was stated several times in this book, the majority of individuals today entering retirement and, certainly, the vast majority of Boomers moving toward retirement, plan to work in some capacity in their retirement years. You were asked to examine what you want more of and less of in retirement. You listed these items in the **Summary of Decisions** at the end of the Chapter on "Work is No Longer Work." Additionally, you were asked to consider your competencies and the work environment you would ideally seek or choose to avoid. Review your earlier work and now answer the following questions to more clearly define your plans for work in retirement:

To what extent do I plan to work in retirement, e.g. full time, part time, occasionally on a project basis, etc.?

_____
_____
_____
_____

What do I plan to derive from my work?   Is earning money the key? Or is it to fulfill a sense of identity or status? Is it my passion? Do I have significant goals that I want to accomplish? Or is work a means toward filling my leisure time or to balance my life? Or is it to enrich my relationships, or to give something to others or the community?   Do I perhaps want to combine some of these needs, and, if so, which aspects stand out as being most important?

_____
_____
_____
_____
_____

If making money is an important product of work, how much money am I seeking to receive? To what extent will it fill a financial need I will have?

_____
_____
_____
_____
_____

Given a choice, what would I ideally like to accomplish from working? Will working serve to provide me with a new identity? How will others, whose opinions I value, see my work?

_____

_____

_____

_____

_____

What do I have to do now or in the near future to prepare myself for a new work routine or occupation in retirement? When does this need to be planned for? When should I actually be preparing for this retirement work, and what do I need to do and with whom do I need to discuss this?

_____

_____

_____

_____

How long, or until what age do I see myself working?
Answer_____

Now, examine the 3 "Key Decisions" I noted on the "Summary of Decisions" page at the conclusion of Chapter 6 – Path 6 (page 185.) To which 3 Key Decisions did I commit? Think about the extent to which these 3 Key Decisions are built into my thoughts above. Are there other thoughts, ideas, research, that I noted in Chapter 6 that need to be pursued beyond what I wrote above in this Action Plan? Do I need to take any additional action?

_____

_____

_____

_____

_____

Chapter 7 – Path 7: Time to Do Good...And for Good Times

In the Chapter, "Time to Do Good...And For Good Times", you had an opportunity to examine how you planned to use your leisure time. Was it to be used in order to find greater fulfillment? Is volunteering one way to find greater fulfillment, or a sense of achievement, or, perhaps, provide some extra "pocket change?" Do you hope to travel, play golf or exercise, enroll in new learning opportunities, share wonderful moments with those whom you most love or care for, or simply relax?

As was pointed out earlier in this book, retirement often is a time when work occupies less structured time than it did before; and we are faced with the "challenge" of more leisure time. Some take to this new allocation of time as "fish to water," reveling in the opportunity. Others (especially career–driven individuals) find the availability of this new leisure time to be very disconcerting, especially if it is accompanied by losing one's occupational identity. Unfortunately, in some of these cases, a level of depression can set in until the individual chooses to define some new "meaningful" activities. This is why Dr. George Vaillant, the author of *Aging Well*, stated that one of the great failings of American companies is in not helping individuals prepare for coping with their new-found leisure time.

Please take a moment to re-examine your earlier completed exercises and answer the following questions:

What do I consider the 5 best uses of my leisure time when I retire, and why?

1._____
_____
_____

2._____
_____
_____

3._____
_____
_____

4._____
_____
_____

5._____
_____
_____
_____

What (if anything) do I need to do to prepare for using the leisure time activities I indicated above? Whom else do I have to involve in my plans? What are the consequences of my not planning for this before confronting all this leisure time?

_____
_____
_____
_____
_____
_____

Because most Boomers plan to work in retirement, did you consider your passion, as well as your hobbies, and the skills and experience you have acquired as new sources of income? For example, the hobby of collecting antiques, or skills such as stage acting, investing, doing magic tricks could lead to a new career and source of income. If so, what would your skills, hobbies and experience be; and what could you derive from these, such as income, fulfillment, a legacy, etc.?

	SKILLS/ HOBBIES	POSSIBLE OUTCOMES
Examples:	Gardening	Become a master gardener and consultant
	Photography	Become an illustrator, leave a legacy
	Doing yoga	Become a fitness instructor
	Collecting war memorabilia	Sell at flea markets and on E-bay
	Plumbing business/retired	Manage a Home Depot hardware section
	Camping/fishing	Sell outdoor equipment at REI

Your own examples and outcomes:

_____   _____
_____   _____
_____   _____

Now, examine the 3 "Key Decisions" I noted on the "Summary of Decisions" page at the conclusion of Chapter 7 – Path 7 (page 219.) To which 3 Key Decisions did I commit? Think about the extent to which these 3 Key Decisions are built into my thoughts above. Are there other thoughts, ideas, research, that I noted in Chapter 7 that need to be pursued beyond what I wrote above in this Action Plan? Do I need to take any additional action?

_____
_____
_____
_____
_____

Chapter 8: Putting It All Together: Your Action Plan

Finally, I come to the point of putting my hard work all together. I need to remember that change is a constant in life and in the universe in which we all live. As they say, "When the rubber meets the road, the best of plans often need changing or more refinement."

The following are the most important facts I discovered or learned about myself and/or my situation:

1._____
_____
_____
2._____
_____
_____
_____
3._____
_____
_____
4._____
_____
_____
5._____
_____
_____

The following are the most important accomplishments I want to achieve in my retirement years:

1._____
_____
_____
2._____
_____
_____
3._____
_____
_____
4._____
_____
_____
5._____
_____
_____

The following are the most significant actions I will need to take to have a most happy or fulfilling retirement. In considering these actions, remember to identify benchmark dates when these should be looked at or completed:

1._____
_____
_____When?_____
2._____
_____
_____When?_____
3._____
_____
_____When?_____
4._____
_____
_____When?_____
5._____
_____
_____When?_____

The following are the most important people that I need to speak with about my retirement plans, and the reasons why they are important:

1._____

_____

_____

2._____

_____

_____

3._____

_____

_____

4._____

_____

_____

5._____

_____

_____

As I steer around the next curve into the future, I need to remember key landmarks or the "guiding principles" that I want to follow in arriving at the most successful retirement lifestyle I can have. Guiding principles are sets of beliefs that influence how I will behave when faced with problem-solving or decision-making throughout my life. As changes occur over time these guiding principles will lead the way and I must remind myself to adhere to these principles:

1._____

_____

_____

2._____

_____

_____

3._____

_____

_____

4._____

_____

_____

5._____

_____

_____

CONGRATULATIONS. If you have taken the time to read and complete the materials in "Customizing Your Retirement," then you are well on your way to fulfilling your retirement goals. Entering retirement is just another important transition in your life's journey. By planning ahead, you have taken a very large step toward making your future more significant and satisfying.

FUTURE STEPS

Please remember to revisit this material from time-to-time and, as indicated above by you, revisit the extent to which you are tracking along on your retirement journey.

TIPS

How do I know when I have arrived? What were some key benchmarks? Can I list the benchmarks or milestones and be able to gauge if I am on track over the course of the first few years?

Year-end 1 following Retirement	Year-end 3 following Retirement.	Year-end 5 following Retirement
Benchmark:	Benchmark:	Benchmark:
Benchmark:	Benchmark:	Benchmark:
Benchmark:	Benchmark:	Benchmark:

Now that you have explored the 7 Paths, you should be better prepared to pursue possibilities, choices and your future happiness.

Good luck and the best of tidings on your life's journey.

Dee and Don

INDEX

Bibliography

- Bland, Warren R., *Retire in Style: 60 Outstanding Places Across the USA and Canada,* © 2005, Next Decade Inc.
- Bland, Warren R., *Retire in Style: 60 Outstanding Places Across America,* © 2001, Next Decade Inc.
- Bratter, Bernice and Helen Dennis, *Project Renewment: the First Retirement Model for Career Women,* Scribner, 2008.
- Bolles, Richard N. and John E. Nelson, *What Color is Your Parachute? for Retirement—Planning Now for the Life You Want,* © 2007 Ten Speed Press.
- Boyles, Denis, "Pessimists Who Think Life Can Only Get Worse Can Only be Right," *AARP Magazine,* March 2007, pages 108, 110-111.
- Bridges, William, *Transitions: Making Sense of Life's Changes,* © 2004, DaCapo Press, Perseus Books.
- Candy, Philip C. and Stephen D. Brookfield, *Self-Direction for Lifelong Learning: A Comprehensive Guide to Theory and Practice,* © 1991, Jossey-Bass.
- Cavellaro, Michaela, "Retire Right," *Priority Magazine,* May/June 2007, pages 30 and 31.
- Davidson, Charlie, "In the Service of Baby Boomers: A Seismic Mind Shift for Financial Service Providers," The CPA Journal, *Online,* a Publication of the New York State Society of CPAs.
- Dychtwald, Ken and Daniel J. Kadlec, *The Power Years: A User's Guide to the Rest of your Life,* © 2005, John Wiley & Sons.
- Freedman, Marc, *PrimeTime: How Baby Boomers will Revolutionize Retirement and Transform America,* © 1999, Perseus Books.
- Freedman, Marc, *Encore: Finding Work that Matters in the Second Half of Life,* © 2007, Perseus Books.
- Galinsky, Ellen, President of the Families and Work Institute and Boston College's Center on Aging and Work, New York, a study, December 2005.
- Goodman, Jordan E., "Debt Relief: Beware the Frauds," *AARP Newsletter,* May-June 2007, pages 48 and 53.
- Hebeler, Henry K., *Getting Started in a Financially Secure Retirement* © 2007, Wiley & Sons.
- Holtzman, Elizabeth, "The Emotional Aspects of Retirement," an article by Elizabeth Holtzman, a counselor in the Faculty and Staff Assistance Program at Amherst College, Massachusetts.
- Hudson, Frederick M., *The Adult Years: Mastering the Art of Self-Renewal,* Revised Edition, page 217 Jossey-Bass Publishers, San Francisco, 1999.
- Johnson, Richard, PhD, *The New Retirement,* First Edition © 2001. www.retirementoptions.com 636-458-0813.
- Koff, Art, *Invent Your Retirement: Resources for the Good Life,* © 2006, Oakhill Press. Chart: "Average Expenditures for Americans" by age group, page 23.
- Konrad, Welecia, "Avoid These Money Traps," *The AARP Magazine,* July & August, 2007, page 35.

- Mahoney, Sarah, "The New Housemates," *AARP the Magazine,* July/August, 2007.
- McMillon, Bill, Doug Cutchins, Anne Geissinger and Ed Asner, *Volunteer Vacations: Short Term Adventures that Will Benefit You and Others,* a guidebook, © Chicago Review Press, 2006.
- Nedelman, Deborah, Ph.D., *"Can Your Relationship Survive Retirement?"* found in www.letlifein.com.
- Paul, Marla, *The Friendship Crisis: Making and Keeping Friends When You're Not a Kid Anymore,* © 2005, Rodale Books.
- Peale, Dr. Norman Vincent, *The Power of Positive Thinking*, originally published in 1952, updated frequently, most recent edition © 2007.
- Post, Stephen, PhD. And Jill Neimark, *Why Good Things Happen to Good People,* © 2008, Broadway Books.
- Sadler, William Alan and William A. Sadler, *The Third Age: Six Principles for Personal Growth and Rejuvenation after Forty,* © 2000, Perseus Publishing.
- Savage, Terry, *The Savage Number: How Much Money Do You Need to Retire,* © 2007, John Wiley & Sons.
- Savageau, David, *Retirement Places Rated: What You need to Know to Plan the Retirement You Deserve,* © Wiley Publishing Inc, 2007, 7th edition.
- Sedlar, Jeri and Rick Miners, *Don't Retire, Rewire: 5 Steps to Fulfilling Work that Fuels Your Passion, Suits Your Personality or Fills Your Pocket,* © 2003, Alpha Books.
- Seibert, Eugene H. and Seibert, Joanne, "Retirement: Crisis or Opportunity," *Personnel Administrator*, August 1986, pages 43-49.
- Tyson, Eric, "Investing for Dummies," *The AARP Magazine*, March-April, 2007.
- Vaillant, George, M.D., *Aging Well: surprising Guideposts to a Happier Life from the Landmark Harvard Study of Adult Development* © 2002, Little, Brown & Co.
- Walker, Jean Erickson, Ed.D, CMF, *The Age Advantage: Making the Most of Your Mid-Life Career Transition* © 2000, Berkley Books.
- Yogev, Sara, *For Better or For Worse…But Not for Lunch: Making Marriage Work in Retirement,* © 2002, Contemporary Books, a Division of McGraw-Hill.

OTHER RESOURCES:

- American Psychological Association.
- Boston College Center for Retirement Research on the web site from Boston College.
- Employee Benefit Research Institute (EBRI), Washington, D.C., *"Notes" Newsletter,* Vol. 24, No. 12, December 2003 and *"Facts from EBRI"* publication, February 2005.

- Employee Benefit Research Institute (EBRI), Retirement Confidence Survey, 2007.
- Employee Benefit Research Institute (EBRI), Retirement Confidence Survey, 2007, Matthew Greenwald and Associates.
- *Kiplinger Magazine,* March 2003, "Will This be Your Next Job…Temporary Work Let's You be a free Agent Without Running a Business," pgs. 83, 84.
- "Life Expectancy Tables," adapted from www.annuityadvantage.com. These tables are compiled from information published by the Office of the Actuary of the Social Security Administration.
- Merrill Lynch, *The New Retirement Survey,"* 2005, "Planning Your Future: Life, Work and Relationships after 50," 2005 Ceridian Corporation.
- National Council on Aging: "Respectability"—New initiative will promote older Americans as "Untapped Resource" to help renew communities.
- NHIS (National Health Interview Survey), NCHS (National Center for Health Statistics).
- National Institute on Aging (NIA).
- National Reverse Mortgage Lenders Association.
- *"Companies Find Rehiring Retirees Creates More Experienced Staff,"* Pittsburgh Business Times, © June 1, 2007. All rights reserved. Reprinted with permission.
- Principal Financial Well-Being Index™ Survey, (http://www.principal.com/wellbeing/index.htm).
- www.seniorjournal.com.
- Three River Workforce Investment Board.
- "Climb Ev'ry Mountain" by Richard Rodgers & Oscar Hammerstein II, Copyright © 1959 by Richard Rodgers and Oscar Hammerstein II. Copyright Renewed WILLIAMSON MUSIC owner of publication and allied rights throughout the World. International Copyright Secured. All rights reserved. Used by Permission.
- US Army Research Institute for the Behavioral and Social Sciences: "The Application of a Model of Adaptive Performance to Army Leader Behaviors," May 2007.
- US Department of Labor, Bureau of Labor Statistics.
- Watson Wyatt Worldwide.
- Yahoo.com's encyclopedia "On Health": "Sexuality and Physical Changes with Age."
- Holmes, Dr. Thomas and Dr. Richard Rahe, studies on the relationship between stress and health.

FOR MORE INFORMATION:

You may find these websites useful:

The Financial Picture:

www.nfcc.org National Foundation for Credit Counseling, 800-388-2227
www.aiccca.org Association of Independent Consumer Credit Counseling Agencies, 800-450-1794
www.annuityadvantage.com Life expectancy tables and annuity information
bulletin.aarp.org/yourmoney/ --AARP Retirement Calculator
www.dividedwefail.org To share your story about economic security
www.ssa.gov/gethelp1.htm To learn more about Social Security benefits
www.businessweek.com Learn the retirement terms you need to know and take a retirement readiness quiz. Also watch a video interview about target-date investing with the head of the retirement business at Barclay's Global Investors.

Keeping in Shape:

www.principal.com/wellbeing/index.htm
www.MyPyramid.gov Food-related information, diets
www.realage.com A diet and nutrition plan tailored to you
www.ADA.org American Dental Association, connections between good dental health and avoiding disease
www.livingto100.com Life Expectancy Calculator
www.Americanheart.org Information on risk factors for heart disease and tips on lowering risk
www.quitnet.org and www.lungusa.org Help in quitting smoking for yourself or others. One-third of smokers eventually die of smoke-related illnesses.
www.weightwatchers.com
www.NutriSystems.com
www.Jennycraig.com
www.seattlesutton.com
www.seniorjournal.com Information on dementia and Alzheimer's
www.WebMD.com A comprehensive site offering medical and health related information
www.aarp.org/bulletin To learn more about the cost of medical care
www.patientadvocate.org Assists individuals in finding medical care when other avenues to care have not been successful
http://www.healthinsuranceinfo.net To find information and health insurance options and state insurance rules
www.unlimitedloveinstitute.com, Stephen Post, PhD., Case Western Reserve University, Cleveland, Ohio
www.retirementwellbeing.org Richard N. Bolles and John E. Nelson, *What Color is Your Parachute? for Retirement—Planning Now for the Life You Want,* © 2007 Ten Speed Press.

Being at Home:

www.findyourspot.com Information on housing locations
www.neighborhoodscout.com Information on housing options
www.bestplaces.net Information on housing locations
www.homestore.com Helps you compare costs of living between locations with the "Moving Calculator"
www.BusinessWeekTV.com -- For more on retiring in your current home, remodeling, or downsizing, watch BusinessWeekTV; to see video clips or find your local station and airtime by zip code.

Work is No Longer Work:

www.aarp.org Has a good section on careers and community service.
http://www.retiredbrains.com/
(best free job search site for 60+ age group)
http://www.retirementjobs.com
(largest job board for older workers
http://www.seniors4hire.org/
(good career site)
http://www.retireecareers.com/
(good career research site)
http://www.yourencore.com/
(research/technical jobs only)
http://www.seniorjobbank.org/links/
(important links for seniors)
http://www.jobsforretirees.com/
(subsidiary of Executive Search Online)
http://www.seniorjobbank.org/
(lots of résumés)
http://www.grayhairmanagement.com/
(executives and managers)
http://www.seniorhelpwanted.com/
http://www.seniorsjobs.com/
http://www.experienceworks.org/
http://www.theretiredworker.com
http://www.ncoa.org/
(National Council on Aging)
http://www.edd.ca.gov/eddswtx.htm
(State of California)
   Here's how this site works.
    1. Start at main page: http://www.ca.gov
    2. Select: Labor and Employment
    3. Select: Targeted Services for Older Workers and
       Women
    4. Reach numerous site links

www.Bulletin.aarp.org – to learn how people are coping with delayed retirement.

Time to Do Good…And for Good Times:

www.aarp.org Has a good section on careers and community service.
www.retire2enjoy.com Has an entire section on the psychology of retirement and lists books on this subject.
www.escus.org Executive Service Corps Affiliate Network (provides senior-level consultants for non-profits, schools and government agencies)
www.score.org Score (offers expertise to help small businesses through nearly 400 chapters)
www.onlinevolunteering.org UN Volunteers (through the U.N. locate volunteer projects that allow you to work online)
www.serviceleader.org Service Leader (click on "for volunteers" for a list of U.S. and international groups)
www.volunteermatch.org Volunteer Match (Comprehensive site for searching all types of volunteer slots throughout the U.S.)
www.crossculturalsolutions.org (Offer work and cultural-exchange opportunities in 12 nations—800-380-4777)
www.vfp.org Volunteers for Peace (802-259-2759)
www.globalvolunteers.org Global Volunteers (has programs in the U.S. and 18 other countries—800-487-1047)
www.habitat.org Habitat for Humanity (sends teams around the world through its Global Village Program—800-422-4828)
Projects Abroad (does everything from conservation work to archaeology projects in 20 countries—888-839-3535);
www.unitedplanet.org United Planet (runs projects in over 50 nations—800-292-2316; i to i
www.itoi.com (800-985-4864)

Miscellaneous:

www.hqda.army.mil/ari/surveys/index.shtml Information on survey by US Army Research Institute for the Behavioral and Social Sciences

Note from the Authors:

The preceding list is for information purposes only. The authors do not recommend or guarantee the content or advice given on any of these links. This is only for the information of our readers and may prove to be helpful in the planning process. We would appreciate hearing from you about the usefulness of any of these sites.

AUTHORS

Diane (Dee) Burman is Co-Founder and Director of the RetireRight Center in Chicago, a non-profit organization devoted to educating pre- and post-retirees in the "Art of Retirement." The focus is on the non-financial aspects of retirement. Before the advent of the RetireRight Center, Ms. Burman founded and acted as principal of an independent human resources consulting firm. Previous to establishing her own company, she was engaged by 3 international corporations for over 25 years, where she worked as an internal consultant and supported projects in management development, executive coaching, team building, diversity management, quality improvement initiatives, career planning, career coaching and redeployment. Ms. Burman was also founder and first President of the Organization Development Network of Chicago. She holds a B.A. from Vassar College and an M.A. from Middlebury College Graduate School of French in France.

Donald Strauss is a career and change management consultant, having worked in the human resources and organization development/change management fields in Fortune 100 companies for over 40 years. Mr. Strauss's wide-ranging responsibilities included oversight of succession planning, management and leadership development, high potential development, and Training & Development. While active as a consultant with a large consulting firm, Mr. Strauss had clients that included Fortune 100 companies, non-profits and municipalities. He is currently on the staff of the RetireRight Center. He also teaches graduate school programs in human resources and career management at Benedictine University. Mr. Strauss has a B.A. from NYU and an M.A. in Labor/Industrial Relations from the University of Illinois. Mr. Strauss has recently been inducted into Sigma Beta Delta, the international Business and Management Honor Society.